Encountering Signs of Faith

"Sometimes a vivid and powerful story lingers in our hearts, long after the 'lesson' is forgotten. But in Allison Gingras's new book, *Encountering Signs of Faith*, the stories and lessons are unforgettably intertwined. With the vigor and conviction of a great faith, Gingras captivates the reader with enthralling true tales of the supernatural rhythms of her ordinary Catholic life. Just see if you can put it down!"

Lisa Mladnich
Founder of Amazing Catechists

"Sacramentals help open our eyes, ears, and souls to the greatest parent ever. In her friendly, conversational tone, Allison Gingras skillfully weaves her story with those of the saints, and encourages readers to deepen their own faith lives with special sections at the end of each chapter for study, journaling or prayer, and hands-on activities. Like sacramentals, this book is a blessing."

Melanie Rigney
Author of *Sisterhood of Saints*

"Allison Gingras's faith-filled stories about the Miraculous Medal and other sacramentals inspire me—and I hope will inspire you—to weave these devotions into family life in a whole new way. Her testimony is real, refreshing, and relatable. For Gingras, sacramentals are a deeply personal and inspiring way to connect with the living God each and every day. Pick up a copy—you won't be disappointed."

Michele Faehnle
Coauthor of *Divine Mercy for Moms*

"In *Encountering Signs of Faith*, Allison Gingras shares a moving account of her use of sacramentals and religious symbols to impart the Catholic faith to her adopted daughter from China who also happens to be profoundly deaf. It is informative and instructive, yet much more. It is at its heart the story of an intimate journey nourished by love and a passion for the faith."

Bishop Edgar M. da Cunha
Diocese of Fall River

"Allison Gingras beautifully unites us as a faithful family by introducing us to people, places, and things that make God's love real. In *Encountering Signs of Faith*, we meet men and women from around the world who embraced sacramentals and lived holy and venerable lives. And, we see how the tangibles of our faith invoke the prayer of the entire Church and help us live the plan of sheer goodness God has for each of us."

From the foreword by **Kelly M. Wahlquist**
Founder of WINE: Women In the New Evangelization

Encountering Signs of Faith

My Unexpected Journey
with Sacramentals, the Saints,
and the Abundant Grace of God

Allison Gingras

AVE MARIA PRESS AVE Notre Dame, Indiana

© 2022 by Allison Gingras

All rights reserved. No part of this book may be used or reproduced in any manner whatsoever, except in the case of reprints in the context of reviews, without written permission from Ave Maria Press®, Inc., P.O. Box 428, Notre Dame, IN 46556, 1-800-282-1865.

Founded in 1865, Ave Maria Press is a ministry of the United States Province of Holy Cross.

www.avemariapress.com

Paperback: ISBN-13 978-1-64680-141-1

E-book: ISBN-13 978-1-64680-142-8

Cover image "Become Rich in What Matters to God" © Jen Norton, jennortonartstudio.com.

Cover and text design by Brianna Dombo.

Printed and bound in the United States of America.

Library of Congress Cataloging-in-Publication Data is available.

Contents

Foreword

Kelly M. Wahlquist

On any random day, and I mean random, in the late eighties and early nineties, something akin to a miracle would happen—I would go to daily Mass. Though raised Catholic and attending a Catholic college, I was far from practicing my faith. It was indeed a miracle if I made it into a church on Sundays, much less attended daily Mass. But, every once in a great while, something drew me there, and truth be told, it wasn't too bad. Classes let out at 11:50 a.m., Mass was at noon, and the cafeteria, across campus from the chapel, closed at 1:00 p.m. That meant Mass was fast! In fact, we called it "low impact aerobics"—stand, sit, stand, sit, stand, kneel, stand, kneel, stand, cross yourself (upper body workout) . . . run to the cafeteria (cardio)!

I recognize two things as I look back to the good old days of my haphazard, though mildly athletic, college Mass attendance. First, a lot is going on in the Catholic Church. It's a busy place to be! We have bells, smells, water, oils, saints, statues, crosses, candles, mystics, medals, prayer cards, penance, and popes. We have relics of dead people and rituals and readings that follow a liturgical year, and we even have a unique and different vocabulary. Don't believe me? Ask a stranger, "Do you know where I can get a good chalice, paten, and ciborium set? And if there is a monstrance that matches, that would be great too."

The second realization of my reflecting upon my youthful days is that God loves us so much that he uses everything—every time, every place, every person, *everything*—to get us to seek him, know him, and love him. He calls us, *all of us*, as adopted sons and daughters, into his family, the Church. To unite his adopted children as a family, God sent his Son to redeem and save us, and he gave us the Holy Spirit, making us heirs to his blessed life. How awesome is that! Truth be told, I didn't get that awesome "a-ha" moment of revelation at one of the fast Masses in college, but I see now how at that time, seeds were planted, and the Divine Gardener was clandestinely cultivating my soul. For God has a plan of sheer goodness. (See *CCC* 1.)

I have to laugh at how God, not only the Divine Gardener but the Divine English Teacher, perfectly uses nouns to bring me closer to him. People, places, and things that have crossed my path draw me into a deeper, more intimate relationship with him. Allison is one of those people, Rome is one of those places, and sacramentals (another great Catholic vocab word) are some of those things.

One Advent, after Allison had posted multiple pictures of squirrels on social media, I decided that I would say a prayer for her whenever I saw a squirrel. This made for a lovely reminder to pray for my friend. Then, spring came, and I understood what St. Paul meant when he said, "pray without ceasing!" It's funny; I used to read that scripture and be somewhat frustrated thinking, "how can I possibly pray without ceasing?" One day, I realized I couldn't, but *we* can. We, the Church, the Body of Christ— together, we can pray without ceasing. This is the beauty of the Liturgy of the Hours: At absolutely every moment, one of our brothers or sisters in Christ is praying the prayer of the Church. United as a family, our prayers never cease.

Aside from my friendship with Allison (and her fondness for squirrels), my faith life has been greatly enhanced by sacramentals. Don't worry if you don't fully understand what a sacramental is; I can assure you that there was a time in my life when I didn't either. I think many of us misunderstand what they are and how they enhance our faith journey.

How blessed are we to have a book explaining sacramentals— we don't have to do the mental aerobics to wrap our minds around their power or purpose! Tapping into her English Arts degree, Allison beautifully unites us as a faithful family by introducing us to people, places, and things that make God's love real. In *Encountering Signs of Faith*, we meet men and women from around the world who embraced sacramentals and lived holy and venerable lives. And, we see how the tangibles of our faith invoke the prayer of the entire Church and help us live the plan of sheer goodness God has for each of us.

Sit back, take in these examples, and as Allison opens her heart and home to you through personal and powerful stories, open the ears of your heart to hear the message the Lord has for you about each sacramental. Ask the Holy Spirit, the Lord, the Giver of Life, to help you understand and embrace these wonderful physical signs of the life of grace. Allow Christ to open wide the door to your heart and speak to you through the riches of sacred scripture. In doing so, may you grow in grace, and with renewed confidence and conviction, may you proudly proclaim, "I am an adopted child of God!"

Introduction

My daughter, consider the life of God which is
found in the Church for the salvation and the
sanctification of your soul. Consider the use that
you make of these treasures of grace, of these
efforts of My love.
—*Jesus to St. Faustina* (Diary, *1758*)

Adoption, Saints, and Sacramentals

What kind of book is this?

An adoption story.

Oh, I'm not super interested in adoption stories.

Actually, every Christian has an adoption story—the story of our
adoption through Christ as his brothers and sisters and as children of
the Father and (for Catholics) of Mary. With any adoption come new
traditions, heirlooms, mementos, and memorabilia, and the opportunity to create lasting legacies. Every adoption begins with a con-
scious decision by one or more adults, endures trials and triumphs,
and includes a time of adjustment to being a new family.

My adoption journey has been an entangling, an incredible inter-
section of discovering the beauty of my adoption into a heavenly family while also answering the call to welcome a sweet little girl into
my heart and home. Even when I strayed from my Catholic faith,
there was always a part of me willing to accept God as my Father; the
unique element of my journey back came with discovering Mary as
my spiritual mother.

When I began reading the scriptures, it was not only St. John's
writing but his relationship with the Blessed Mother that would open a
door to my heart I didn't know existed—much like what would happen

when I accepted God's will to expand our family through adoption. Little by little, a parade of saints, whose personal encounters with Mary led to powerful devotions and sacramentals, would enter my life and strengthen my faith. Each devotion and sacramental expanded my idea of what it meant to be Catholic and of the influential role of grace in our lives.

Ours is not a distant or unaware God—he is loving and gives visible signs of his great and eternal love for each and every one of us! These sacred signs that point to the sacraments (from which we receive the graces we need to live the Christian life) are called sacramentals, and they come with spiritual benefits that we receive through the intercession of the Church (visible and invisible). While sacramentals are linked to the prayers of the Church, and blessings are themselves sacramentals, what amazes me is how sacramentals are also silent prayers, ways for us to communicate our faith without speaking a word. The *Catechism of the Catholic Church* tells us:

> Sacramentals do not confer the grace of the Holy Spirit in the way that the sacraments do, but by the Church's prayer, they prepare us to receive grace and dispose us to cooperate with it. "For well-disposed members of the faithful, the liturgy of the sacraments and sacramentals sanctifies almost every event of their lives with the divine grace which flows from the Paschal mystery of the Passion, Death, and Resurrection of Christ. From this source all sacraments and sacramentals draw their power. There is scarcely any proper use of material things which cannot be thus directed toward the sanctification of men and the praise of God. (1670)

Sacramentals are mystical, not magical; reminders, not talismans; and grace avenues, not grace givers. They are beautiful, tangible ways to embrace the abundant grace God has for each of us. Grace, his undeserved yet freely given gift of his Holy Spirit within each of us, helps us follow his will for us, grow in holiness, and continually offer our yes to being his beloved sons and daughters.

The crucifix, Miraculous Medal, and sterling silver scapular dangling from a chain around my neck convey who I am, *whose* I am, and what I believe before I ever say a word. When I wore my brown scapular, someone would often whisper, "Your bra is showing!" to which

I would giggle and kindly respond, "Oh no, that's just my Catholic showing."

Secure in my adoption into the family of God, I found that surrendering to God's will no longer seem scary or impossible. The idea that an anxiety-ridden woman could, through grace, travel to China to bring home a deaf three-year-old became plausible. It was even exciting! As defined in Hebrews 11:1, faith is "the assurance of things hoped for, the conviction of things not seen." The last hurdle to my reversion hinged squarely on the assurance that God is real! I remember sometime early in 2005, begging Jesus, as the centurion did in Mark's Gospel, "I believe; help my unbelief!" (9:24). The answer came slowly but steadily over months and years, as a river of grace flowed through sacraments, sacramentals, scriptures, and saints.

Mary, full of grace, brought to my life encounters with the saints who once encountered her in real, tangible, and powerful ways. She revealed that I too could be filled with the power of God's Holy Spirit within me. Each saint showed me a tangible way to connect to an invisible God I longed to know but struggled to believe in. Adoption can be challenging, but nothing in my life has been more rewarding. The unmistakable parallel between my burgeoning faith and adjustment into my Christian family and our family's journey of adoption was impossible to ignore.

Doing the Extraordinary

Have you ever witnessed Jesus do something amazing in your life or in the life of another? What is your response to being allowed this tremendous privilege? Do you share what you have seen, or do you keep it to yourself? The most potent evangelization is rarely the most eloquent teaching; it is the personal testimony of what Jesus has done in our lives.

In the summer of 2005, as my reversion moved from *maybe I'll allow myself to believe* to *I'm in this for the long haul, Jesus*, I first felt the stirring in my heart that my family was being called to adopt, I instantly knew that it would be a deaf little girl. I never challenged this movement of the Spirit; I just knew. I was so convinced it was true that I immediately signed up for American Sign Language (ASL) classes. To everyone who asked why I was learning, I replied, "I am convinced that God is sending us a little girl who will be deaf, and I want to be prepared."

I recognized I was taking a considerable risk in speaking so boldly about this strange possibility in our lives. If we were not matched with a child with a hearing loss, I could look incredibly foolish, but my courage to speak what I felt was truth could glorify God in a way that nothing before in my life had. Although I fear embarrassment like most people, the reward of sharing how God moves in our everyday lives always outweighed any risk. I continued to learn ASL for three years and to share with others my conviction that the little girl we were waiting for would be deaf.

In February of 2006, we began the formal process of adoption, which included lots of intake paperwork. We didn't fill out any special paperwork to increase the odds of being matched with a little deaf girl; we were open to whichever child the Lord saw fit to bless us with. As biological parents, we believe that God does not make mistakes and that the child he blesses our family with is the child we were meant to have; we entered adoption with this same mindset.

On April 30, 2009, we received the call that we had been matched with a beautiful three-year-old girl who was indeed profoundly deaf. If people thought I was astonished by Jesus's movement in my life before that phone call, there was no shutting me up now! That day the Lord cast the demon of doubt from my heart and showed me his authority over my life, and sharing that never gets old.

This little girl would become our daughter, and we'd name her Faith because it honestly took all the faith in the world for me to see this incredible mission from God through. For the sake of reducing confusion throughout the book, and because this is what we call her at home, I will refer to my sweet kid as *Faithy*, and to the gift God bestows on us of knowing and believing in him as *faith*.

Teaching the Tangibles of Faith

Teaching the Catholic faith to someone without language was never something I expected to be doing. Catholicism does have its language; even now, I'll have to look up some of the words I come across in my spiritual reading. *Transubstantiation* (yes, I needed spell check on this one), *absolution*, *monstrance*, *hagiographer* (one who chronicles the lives of saints)—these words were not on my SAT list. Once I knew their meanings, however, it brought a whole new dimension to my faith, unfolding before me untold treasures. My only concept of teaching the deaf came from watching *The Miracle Worker*, where Annie Sullivan teaches Helen Keller about water. Yet techniques depicted in the film gave me great insights on how we might expose Faithy to the unseen through the use of her other senses.

What Helen could feel, with words to eventually match, would make her world more real and open up unique opportunities for to communicate to the world. That was one of the things about my daughter that amazed me—that she'd gone three years without really being able to articulate how she felt, what she knew, and—most important—what she wanted to know. What an incredible responsibility and gift God was giving my family to share him and the world with her.

The tangibles of our faith make God real to each of us, expanding our knowledge of how much he truly loves us. Well-meaning, brilliant theologians can sometimes leave the very people they are trying to inspire and educate dumbfounded and confused by words they do not know. Listening to a rather popular theologian speak at a conference once, I had to bite my tongue to keep from asking for a Catholic dictionary during his presentation! I took this experience into my teaching of my daughter, remaining careful to introduce things in ways she could understand more clearly—with stories, hands-on activities, and of course many, many visuals.

Hence, the challenge of passing on my faith to my child who lacked words and language for even the simplest things became the perfect occasion for using sacramentals. And along the way, I discovered a breadth and depth of my beloved faith, especially saints and devotions, that I didn't realize existed. For Faithy, we had to figure out creative and innovative ways to spark the head knowledge of God. Incredibly, as my head's knowledge of Catholicism increased, I felt my heart, where I had struggled to place him in the past, respond to God as well. People often joke that the longest journey in the world is getting our faith from our heads into our hearts.

Truth be told, I knew that I wasn't in this alone, that the Holy Spirit was indeed the first and most effective teacher of the faith. I often look at her and think, *What has God taught you that I don't even have a clue about?* And I look forward to the day when her language ability has reached the level where she can begin to share God with me in a whole new way. I have long suspected, especially because of her sweet response to some of our lessons, that the Master Teacher had already explained most of this to her in a way I'll never fully comprehend.

It was not merely her inability to hear but her struggle with comprehension that first frustrated me, but now I recognize it as a blessing because I see what is meant by letting the little children come. Humbling myself to be like a child, not always feeling like I know everything, and being receptive to learning new things opens my heart to receive even more blessings and knowledge of my faith. We serve an unfathomable God, and if we believe one moment that we have learned all there is to know about him, then we are not only missing out but quite honestly foolish. We risk abdicating the abundance of ways that God wants to bless, teach, and comfort us. Most of this book will be about how I've taught Faithy about the Catholic Church and its teachings and traditions, but if I'm honest with myself, she has taught me immeasurably more about the Lord that I love and try to serve.

Throughout this journey, the scripture passage "What no eye has seen, nor ear heard, / nor the heart of man conceived, / what God has prepared for those who love him" (1 Cor 2:9) comforted my insecure mother's heart. Although that passage speaks of heaven, of course, I can't help but recognize in it the tender and mystical way God speaks to those who learn of the world differently than I do, whose senses, if compromised in one way, are intensified in another. Faithy insisted we sit in the front row when I began to interpret the Mass for her into ASL. Faithy explained that moving closer allowed her to see both the altar and my interpretation of the words. Faithy is fascinated by the consecration and will often tell me to stop interpreting the music so she can pay attention to what the priest or deacon (especially when the deacon of the day is her dad) is doing on the altar. Last, her love for prayer, spiritual events, and holy objects is quite enviable—I often watch her and think, *What was I worried about?*—yet as you will see, there were a few hiccups.

Sacramentals—tangible comforts such as my Miraculous Medal, scapular, and the smiling faces of the saints covering my desk—played an enormous role in my reversion back to the Catholic faith. Each one serves a specific role in how my soul is prepared to receive the grace necessary to follow Christ. The scapular and my rosary offer protection and comfort as I lean on my heavenly mother, Mary. There is holy water throughout my home and even holy oils such as St. André Bessette's St. Joseph oil from Montreal to bless myself and my children.

Sacramentals invoke the prayer of the entire Church, much as we live the truth of these two scripture passages: "Two are better than one, because they have a good reward for their toil. For if they fall, one will lift up his fellow; but woe to him who is alone when he falls and has not another to lift him up. Again, if two lie together, they are warm; but how can one be warm alone? And though a man might prevail against one who is alone, two will withstand him. A threefold cord is not quickly broken" (Eccl 4:9–12) and "Again I say to you, if two of you agree on earth about anything they ask, it will be done for them by my Father in heaven. For where two or three are gathered in my name, there am I in the midst of them" (Mt 18:19–21).

As a daughter of God, I have been so blessed to observe these physical signs of the life of grace help me in times when the unseen world of faith felt too elusive for me to grasp. Before I uncovered the bounty of sacramentals and devotions, my life felt like building castles in the sand in the hope of creating a permanent home. Every wave of uncertainty washed those castles away until I established a firm foundation on the truth, beauty, and faithfulness of the Church (see Matthew 7:26–27). The unexpected cementing came via guiding my daughter to use these faith tools that are discernible to her through sight and touch.

As our family navigated life with Faithy, the idea of being created in God's likeness and image made us realize that all our senses could play an essential role in our growing ever closer to him. He is not a God who wants to be distant; the scriptures talk about how he collects our tears (see Psalm 56:8) and knows the number of hairs on our heads (see Matthew 10:30, Luke 12:7). These examples show a Father who clearly wants to know, love, and guide his children through and throughout the moments of our ordinary everyday lives. It is that journey I wish to share with you.

Chapter Features

The turning point of my reversion back to practicing the Catholic faith came as I began to incorporate scripture in my prayer life, attend small-group study, and learn how to put my faith into action. These actions led me to discover fascinating stories of saints' lives and Marian apparitions, and the powerful sacramentals and faith-building devotions they inspired. My experience with adopting these signs of faith has inspired a section at the end of each chapter to help you mine more deeply the grace waiting for you in each of the sacramentals and devotions shared in this book, as well as to encourage you to encounter Christ in valuable and poignant ways.

Included in each *Adopting a More Tangible Faith* section is a **Growing in Grace with Scripture** segment to nurture a connection between the sacramental and/or devotion, the story of encounter, and scripture. I hope this helps you adopt these devotions in a more meaningful way into your personal faith journey. **Uncovering Grace** offers questions for you to contemplate in private or use with others. One of the greatest blessings of connecting with others to discuss spiritual matters comes from how everyone experiences the world so uniquely. I love listening to the different perspectives of my "Bible Babes," as I affectionately refer to them. Inevitably one of the ladies offers a perspective I missed in reading the material on my own. I've learned after fifteen years of participating in small-group study that faith shared multiplies the blessings.

Last, I've included **Grace-Building Activities** to help you build a more tangible faith—not just one read, studied, or even discussed, but one that sparks action. Perhaps as one who learns best with hands-on activities, teaching Faithy with these kinds of lessons not only strengthened her faith but tightened our bond. I share the ideas that helped solidify our experiences of faith, and I believe they will do the same for you and your family.

I invite you to lean into the grace, promises, blessings, and prayers of the Church, so that you may embrace and live the faith all of these beautiful devotions and sacramentals claim for you.

All about Grace

St. Catherine Labouré and the Miraculous Medal

Grace is not a strange, magic substance which is subtly filtered into our souls to act as a kind of spiritual penicillin. Grace is unity, oneness within ourselves, oneness with God.

—*Thomas Merton*

Meeting the Miraculous Medal

Admiring the shiny, oval medal around my friend's neck, I commented on how pretty I found this delicate, unique piece of jewelry. Chuckling, with a soft kindness, without an air of condescension, she removed the emblem for what I thought was an opportunity to give me a closer look. I rubbed my fingers over the raised image of Mary on front of the medal, contemplating the numerous rays emulating from her fingers, then flipping it over to ponder the meaning of the "t" sitting atop an "M," both resting upon two hearts. "This," my friend finally interjected into the silence, "is a Miraculous Medal, and I want you to have it." Although I tried to refuse it and hand the medal back, she shook her head, insisting she was merely following the promptings of the Holy Spirit. She told me when I got home to look up the story, the promises, and the blessings that came with wearing a Miraculous Medal, which of course I did, and now some twenty years later, there is always one around my neck. Interestingly, years later, I would do the same when questioned about the medal—feel the nudge of the Holy Spirit to pass that original medal to another seeking to know the abundance of God's grace.

The Trouble with Unused Gifts

One Christmas, my sister gave me a Wii Fit. At first, I was a wee bit angry because maintaining a healthy weight and exercising have been a lifelong struggle for me. My immediate reaction to the gift was to be insulted and to make a secret vow never to use it. As I received and opened the present I honestly never intended to use, I thought, *How dare she point out where I need to make a change in my life?*

After she left, I shoved the console and all its accoutrements into the closet. Soon after, I learned that my mother's type 2 diabetes now required daily insulin shots. At the same time, my father, who had had his first heart attack at thirty-four and a heart transplant at fifty-five, began a new battle with congestive heart failure. Both of my parents' conditions, which can be inherited, are also conditions that studies show can be avoided by maintaining proper diet and exercise—exercise, like that encouraged by the fun and low-impact Wii Fit my sweet baby sister had just gifted me!

I realized that my sister's gift had nothing to do with physical appearance. She was not commenting on my size or shape. Her gift came solely from a place of deep and abiding love for me. The gift was meant to give me a fighting chance at a full, wonderful life courtesy of a strong, healthy, and (hopefully) disease-free inside!

I misunderstood the intentions of God and his gift of grace in my life as well. I automatically assumed that the commandments, the "rules and regulations" of the Catholic faith, and the idea that God has a plan for my life were in place to tell me what to do. These "gifts" felt oppressive to me, and I failed to see God's compassion within them. As with my misinterpretation of my sister's gift, pride was blinding me from seeing the desire for my well-being overflowing in each of God's gifts. God bestows faith, mercy, and especially grace generously on us, without cost, for one simple reason: "God is love" (1 Jn 4:8).

Everything God asks of us is ordered toward our good, our salvation, and his desire to have us in heaven with him forever. His gifts provide us the means to have strong, healthy, and virtuous insides. His gifts are soul food, and we can consume as much of them as we want and never worry about becoming too, let's say, fluffy. But for these magnificent graces to be useful in our lives, we need to be willing to receive, open, and use them. God is never outdone in his generosity. We are the fool-hearted who neglect to embrace all he has for us.

The Blessed Mother appeared to St. Catherine Labouré and described the various elements of the "Miraculous Medal" image. The rays emanating from Mary's hands, which Catherine described as brilliant and dazzling, according to the Blessed Mother, "symbolize the graces I shed upon those who ask for them. The gems from which rays do not fall are the graces for which souls forget to ask."[1] Imagine all that abundant grace, as symbolized by the illuminated rays from her hands, available from God for all people, unused by a world in such need of it; this extraordinary gift languishing because people fail to see their great need for it.

God's grace is freely given, a total bargain—since when did we stop loving a bargain? Yet the world disregards this generous gift, unaware of the goodness behind its offering, much as I first did with the Christmas Wii!

Finding Faith

After only a year in the Bible study group, God's grace opened my heart to hear his calling our family to adoption. After years of discerning continually in prayer if or how to expand our family, I began to feel a strong call to the idea of adoption. Although I had become pregnant four times, the two pregnancies between the births of my sons were a near-fatal ectopic pregnancy and then a miscarriage. Although we were open to life and to God's will, I was nervous about another pregnancy.

I'd not thought of adoption since the day in eighth grade nearly thirty years earlier, when, after falling in love with ASL, I ran into the kitchen to announce to my mother my desire to have a child that was deaf. Aware of genetics and even how morose a wish to give birth to a child with a hearing loss of any kind, the idea of adoption began to kindle in my heart. Now, as the adoption issue resurfaced in my mind, my mother reminded me of this childhood wish, and these seemingly crazy desires of my youthful heart began to seem like finding that missing piece of a thousand-piece puzzle. As Psalm 37:4 reminded me, "Take delight in the Lord, / and he will give you the desires of your heart."

Each day I prayed (okay, begged) for clarity on things like where we should adopt from, how would I know which child to choose, and where we would ever find the money. I wasn't at all sure I wanted an infant—while babies themselves are adorable, I was approaching forty and had considerable reluctance to plunge back into infant care with all the diapers, bottles, and sleepless nights.

The more I prayed for clarity and direction, the more the Holy Spirit filled my heart with joy at the idea of adopting a child who was not an infant and most likely would not be able to hear. Following this nudge of the Spirit, my sons and I began taking ASL classes. We had nothing to lose in following this inspiration. In the end, if I had heard correctly, this step of faith would glorify God; if I were wrong, the boys and I would have learned a beautiful language and filled those long two years of waiting with something fun and valuable.

A year into the adoption process, we received a call from the adoption agency informing us they believed they'd found the perfect match for our family—a three-year-old, sweet little girl who was deaf. Due to her deafness, she was living in a foster home rather than an orphanage, in China. The thought of adopting from China—a communist country literally half the world away (which meant a very long flight for this not-so-brave passenger) instilled acute anxiety in me. And yet we could not ignore the many signs that this petrifying adventure was part of a plan God had placed before us.

Even our choice of adoption agency had been carefully orchestrated by God's loving hand. In February 2007, at the time we were considering starting the adoption process, I was running a preschool program in my home. On Friday at pick-up, a parent who had just completed an amazing adoption from Kazakhstan got my attention before leaving with her child. She said, "You are going to think I'm crazy, but I feel like I'm supposed to tell you to consider China Adoption with Love (CAWLI)." She knew our family had begun praying about the possibility of starting our own adoption journey.

The next day, my husband, Kevin, and I spent the day at a team-building meeting. After sharing our crazy high school romance and our journey from being near atheists to a solid Catholic family, we mentioned that we were now considering the possibility of adoption. One of the other team members came up to us and said, "You need to contact CAWLI. It is adoption for dummies. You'll love how easy they make it." I hadn't told him about my conversation with the preschool mom or that we were even considering China.

On Sunday, while I was helping with our church's youth choir, God gave me one more undeniable sign. Excited by the previous two days' signs, I shared with three young Chinese American sisters the possibility of our adopting from China. That evening, one of them emailed that they'd been hired to play their Chinese dulcimers (stringed instruments) at an adoption agency fundraiser. Want to guess which agency? Yes, CAWLI again—and I hadn't mentioned the name of the agency to them!

Kevin and I discussed all the complications an international adoption could entail: large travel and adoption costs, our fear of flying, leaving our boys behind for more than two weeks, and the uncertainty of visiting a communist country. Yet we felt called to follow this path, so we registered with CAWLI. After sixteen months, they reached out to us about a three- (nearly four-) year-old girl in need of a home. Although she was much older than I had anticipated, the minute I saw the photograph of her sweet little face, which oddly resembled my younger son's, I knew she was the child God chose for our family. Now, we had to prepare ourselves for the reality of traveling halfway around the world to China. Funny how grace veiled certain facts, such as that travel would include a total of six flights, three on Chinese airlines! If I had spent any time contemplating the logistics of how we would get this child home, I am not sure I could have followed through with it. I appreciate the grace sufficient in the moment that God promises and clearly delivers!

A Little Miracle in China

On the morning before we finally met Wu Feng Hua (aka Faithy), I woke up with a red, swollen, and terribly painful stye in my eye. I'd never had one before but knew these things don't get better on their own. Panic began to settle in as it worsened throughout the day. As you can imagine, I was nervous about visiting a Chinese doctor since it was the middle of the swine flu epidemic but wanted to get better so I could meet Faithy the following day. My thought all day: *Blessed Mother, I need a miracle.* I didn't have time to be unwell, nor did I feel comfortable seeing a doctor in China; I just wanted to focus on being with my new daughter. Trusting in the power of prayer and the promised graces of the Miraculous Medal, I got on my knees and prayed, confident Mary would help me. I put the medal against my eye—the oval shape fit perfectly—and prayed for intercession and healing, closing with a Memorare and a Hail Mary. Within an hour, my eye was healed!

Grace Abounds for All of Us

Each of us has desires that God longs to fulfill for us. Some are so minute they are fulfilled without our ever recognizing that grace played a role. Sometimes he plants the idea in our hearts early in our lives, like my desire to adopt a child. Other times he works through circumstances to lead us along the right path.

The path God had in mind for us sent us on a mission that took us across a continent and an ocean; your mission is just as important, even if it takes you no further than your kitchen table. Either way, it takes courage to seek and to find the Lord's will for our lives. If your heart is open to what he asks, I can guarantee that God will send you all the graces you need to fulfill his plan for you!

But how do we know when a desire is God's guiding hand and when it is simply something we want for ourselves? How do we know when something is God's will—and when it is our own? How do we discern the Holy Spirit's nudges in our hearts and not confuse them with our will and desires? How do we truly "take delight in the Lord" so that he may "give [us] the desires of [our] heart" (Ps 37:4)? Simply—yet not always so easily—we do so by accepting the gifts of grace that are abundantly and readily available. By participating in the sacraments, spending time with scripture, and communicating with God in prayer, we open the wellspring of graces necessary for navigating this life.

Sacramentals, such as holy cards and medals, can be powerful aids to receiving holy light shining within us to show us the right path. For me, the floodgates of grace opened when I discovered the promises of the Miraculous Medal. Mary's explanation of the dark and light rays[2] awakened in me a desire to never leave grace unclaimed. Every time I look at my little girl, I am reminded of the power of grace and shudder to think of what our family would have missed without her coming into our lives. And what might have become of Faithy, who faced so many challenges (more on those later), had we not obeyed those promptings of the Spirit?

The most important thing is to *place yourself regularly in God's presence* and ask him to show you his plan. Spend time with Jesus in the Word of God and in his eucharistic presence, as did St. Catherine Labouré, whose Miraculous Medal has been a source of great comfort and inspiration to me on my spiritual journey. According to St. Catherine:

> Whenever I go to the chapel, I put myself in the presence of our good Lord, and I say to Him, "Lord, here I am. Tell me what You would have me do." If he gives me some task, I am content and I thank Him. If he gives me nothing, I still thank Him since I do not deserve to receive anything more than that. And then, I tell God everything that is in my heart. I tell Him about my pains and my joys, and then I listen. If you listen, God will also speak to you, for with the good Lord, you have to both speak and listen. God always speaks to you when you approach Him plainly and simply.[3]

St. Catherine Labouré

Catherine Labouré, known to her family as Zoé, was born in Burgundy, France, on May 2, 1806. Tragically, her mother died when she was only nine years old. Following the funeral, Catherine retired to her room, climbed upon a chair, carefully removed the statue of the Blessed Mother from the wall, kissed it, and said: "Now, dear Lady, you are to be my mother."[4]

A dream of St. Vincent de Paul affirmed her desire to enter religious life. Catherine began her novitiate with the Daughters of Charity of St. Vincent de Paul on April 21, 1830, at their convent in Paris, and on January 30, 1831, she took her vows. It was in this convent that Catherine would experience two Marian apparitions.

On the night of July 18, 1830, a beautiful child, dressed in white and emanating heavenly light, awakened Catherine Labouré from her sleep with the words "Sister, sister, sister." She followed the child to the chapel, where all the candles were lit, as if for midnight Mass. Catherine saw a beautiful woman walk in and sit on the chair used by the director of the community. Catherine reported, "I went closer and, throwing myself on my knees, rested my hands on the knees of the Blessed Virgin. At that instant, I tasted the sweetest joy of my life—a delight beyond expression."[5]

In addition to the rays radiating from "Mary's jeweled fingers," Catherine saw an oval appear around the Blessed Mother, with the words "O Mary, conceived without sin, pray for us who have recourse to thee." The word *recourse* can be defined as "a source of help in a difficult situation" as well as "a turning to someone or something for help or protection"; both meanings illuminate the type of relationship Mary longs to have with us—all rooted firmly in the abundant grace of God.

On the reverse side of the medal shown to Catherine in the apparition, was a letter M intersected at the top with a cross and a bar (representing the altars of the world). Underneath was the Sacred Heart of Jesus crowned with thorns and the Immaculate Heart of Mary pierced by a sword. Twelve stars surrounded the entire image. The interweaving of Mary's initial and the cross shows Mary's part in our salvation and her role as Mother of the Church. The twelve stars signify the twelve tribes of Israel and the twelve apostles, who represent the entire Church as it surrounds Mary. They also recall the vision of St. John, writer of the Book of Revelation, in which "a great sign appeared in heaven, a woman clothed with the sun, and the moon under her feet, and on her head a crown of twelve stars" (12:1, NABRE).[6]

The Miraculous Medal

> I knew nothing. I was nothing. For this reason God picked me out.
>
> —St. Catherine Labouré

Mary instructed Catherine to have a medal made according to this model presented in the apparition. Catherine heard Mary say to her, "Everyone who wears it around their neck will receive great graces. Graces will be abundant for those who have confidence." After the medal was fabricated and distributed, many miracles began to be attributed to the graces Mary promised, and the medal, first referred to as the Medal of the Immaculate Conception and the Medal of Our Lady of Graces, would eventually become known as the Miraculous Medal.

The Miraculous Medal is unique as the only medal whose design was provided to us by Mary, under the title of Our Lady of Grace, along with the promise of graces to be bestowed upon those who faithfully wear it.[7]

The Blessed Mother's message to Catherine involved the abundant grace God had available and longed to share with his beloved adopted children. Where in your life could you use an outpouring of grace? In these moments, make a habit of repeating, as many times as you desire, the words engraved on the medal, "O Mary, conceived without sin, pray for us who have recourse to thee." Boldly ask the Blessed Mother to bring your petitions to her Son and to give you the graces necessary to know, accept, and follow God's will in whatever situations you have brought to her.

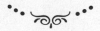

Adopting a More Tangible Faith

Growing in Grace with Scripture

For those who are led by the Spirit of God are children of God. For you did not receive a spirit of slavery to fall back into fear, but you received a spirit of adoption, through which we cry, "Abba, Father!" The Spirit itself bears witness with our spirit that we are children of God, and if children, then heirs, heirs of God and joint heirs with Christ—if, in

fact, we suffer with him so that we may also be glorified
with him. (Rom 8:14–17 NRSVCE)

Sitting on a hillside at a Christian music festival, in July 2007, surrounded by thousands of people, I flipped nervously through the pages
of my Bible seeking affirmation for our recent decision to adopt from
China. As a woman with acute anxiety, I found every aspect of adoption stressful and scary—beginning with where to adopt from and
how to find the money; followed quickly by how, with my paralyzing
fear of flying, I could possibly travel to China; and moving on to my
overwhelming uncertainty regarding how to harmoniously assimilate
her into our family and properly raise her given the language barriers.
Adding to these worries all the insecurities and concerns I held about
my parenting, given the missteps and mistakes I'd already made raising
the boys, I questioned God's plan. How could I reconcile the desire and
conviction I'd felt back in eighth grade with my adult uncertainty as to
whether the grace of God could strengthen me to do what I dreamed?

The above scripture suddenly came into view, and as I read the
words, peace enveloped my whole being. It was not I but God who
would do all of it. By my own adoption into the Christian family, I
could lean into the love of my Abba to accomplish whatever would
be asked of me in this adoption, as well as in all the moments of my
life. Whatever suffering might come would be nothing compared to
the glory that awaits. God chose us to be this little girl's family, and
through cooperation with all the graces he'd shower on us during the
process and beyond, I would embrace and trust in his plan!

Uncovering Grace

1. Think back to all the gifts you've received in your life. Which have
   you treasured the most? Did they come for a special occasion
   when you were expecting a gift, or were they completely unexpected? How about gifts that, although well-meaning, remained
   unused? What lessons drawn from presents received can you apply
   to better accept God's many gifts?
2. Where in your life would you like to see a strengthening of grace?
   Is there a particular relationship or circumstance where you would
   like God to heal and strengthen you? How do sacramentals serve

to remind you that you are not alone and that God gives you all you need to successfully navigate your way through these difficult times?

3. Do you own a Miraculous Medal? If so, how often do you wear it? And when you do, have you experienced the outpouring of graces Mary spoke to St. Catherine about? If you don't wear one, which of the promises shared with Catherine may inspire you to adopt this devotion?

Grace-Building Activities

- Wear the the Miraculous Medal. If you don't already wear a Miraculous Medal around your neck, as Mary requested in her appearances to St. Catherine, consider purchasing one from a local Catholic bookstore (sometimes church or shrine gift shops carry them as well). If you cannot afford one or would like to purchase some in bulk to share with your parish, the Association of the Miraculous Medal (www.amm.org) can assist you. Take advantage of the abundant graces offered through this sacramental.

- Pray the Miraculous Medal Novena for your, or a loved one's, intentions (see appendix). Fr. Joseph A. Skelly, CM, founder of the Central Association of the Miraculous Medal, began the Miraculous Medal Perpetual Novena at the Miraculous Medal Shrine in Philadelphia on Monday, December 8, 1930. The perpetual novena has continued uninterrupted each Monday at the Miraculous Medal Shrine. According to the shrine's website, thousands of people around the world join in praying this novena, either at the shrine, through the internet, or in their parishes.[8] The prayer can be prayed any time, including the traditional novena format of nine days in a row, and is a wonderful activity to tap even deeper into the graces promised through this beautiful devotion.

- Learn about each element of the medal. There are many resources online, including detailed coloring pages that allow you to become acquainted with this precious image given by the Blessed Mother herself while enjoying the relaxation of coloring—especially together with your child (or grandchild).

- Google "Miraculous Medal activities." I particularly like the activities on Catholic Icing (https://www.catholicicing.com/

micaculous-medal-craft-for-catholic-kids), such as creating a tin foil Miraculous Medal replica. Be creative and brainstorm your own way of artistically depicting the medal to enhance your understanding of the medal Mary herself designed.

2

Companions on the Journey

St. Faustina Kowalska and Divine Mercy

Jesus: **My child, life on earth is a struggle indeed; a great struggle for My kingdom. But fear not, because you are not alone. I am always supporting you, so lean on Me as you struggle, fearing nothing. Take the vessel of trust and draw from the fountain of life—for yourself, but also for other souls, especially such as are distrustful of My goodness.**
—*St. Faustina* (Diary, 1488)

My Introduction to Divine Mercy Devotions

I began to better understand the power and beauty of the many Divine Mercy devotions in April of 2009. Leaving Mass one Sunday, I noticed a little pamphlet urging the faithful to say a novena beginning on Good Friday and leading up to Divine Mercy Sunday. Drawn to its promises, I began to pray the Divine Mercy Chaplet daily along with the prescribed prayers, as directed in the pamphlet. I must admit that early in my reversion, I generally sought out holy devotions with promises. They brought me comfort in my anxiety. However, just as the Holy Spirit had used yummy snacks to keep me attending my first Bible study group, he used my weakness for promises to introduce me to what would become lifelong devotions.

The fact that I completed the novena was in itself evidence of divine intervention because I almost never remember to do anything nine days in a row! The efficiency of something as simple as adding prayer to your calendar and setting a three o'clock alarm is incredible. I then attended a Catholic women's conference in Boston on Divine Mercy Sunday, April 16. It was a perfect opportunity not only to solidify the permanent place of this devotion in my life, but also to receive the final affirmation I so desperately needed regarding our plans to adopt.

The affirming words would come from the speaker Kerri Caviezel, who spoke of adopting her older special-needs children from China. I had seen Kerri on an EWTN show a few months earlier, and the similarity of our stories touched my heart. Recognizing and believing the signs God places in our life was foreign to me until, through Kerri's witness, I saw the Spirit clearly at work in and around me.

Kerri described the moments when she'd observed the Spirit at work answering her prayers or questions, some she hadn't yet voiced. Her words fanned my ember of longing for my husband, Kevin, and me to become parents to a special child in need of a home into a flame that would only be extinguished by pursuing this in our lives.

Some signs are subtle, while others are more overt; perhaps both kinds could be brushed off as pure coincidence, but I realized as she spoke that she and I both tended to see these moments as God's presence. For me, a *godcidence* is defined as seeing the world through the eyes of God and appreciating the impeccable timing of the moment, which I couldn't orchestrate no matter how hard I tried. I couldn't have known that day that God would use Kerri as a messenger telling us to trust him in opening our hearts to adopt. With every word of her story, my heart pounded faster and tears welled in my eyes. Nothing compares to feeling the Spirit of God speak directly into your heart and answer a prayer.

In my journal that day, I asked myself the burning question—would I be courageous enough to pray for God to reveal his plans to me, and for the wisdom and conviction to believe and trust in them? St. Paul counsels us to test everything (see 1 Thessalonians 5:21). In addition, I brought my thoughts to my spiritual director, Deacon Jerry

Ryan, to help me discern what might be God's will (and what might be mine). I try never to be overconfident in a sign until the Spirit assures me, often requiring confirmation at least three times before I allow myself to believe and/or move on the Spirit's inspiration.

Kerri had shared that the children her family adopted were older, not infants, which most people picture in adoption. She opened up about her initial concerns, as she saw it unfolding before her and how motherhood would come to her, she knew in her heart and through various signs like special dates and connections to the saints that this was indeed God's will for her family. I too worried about adopting an older child—nearly four is not ancient, but having worked in early education for many years, I knew the significance of the years we'd miss with our child. And although I had my heart set and believed I was being called to adopt a child that was deaf, I still had concerns about how that would play out in our family and whether I was truly qualified to take the best care of her. This is where trust, hope, and faith play the greatest role in our faith life—and in our case, the life of Faithy. The words from Jeremiah 29:11 repeated often through my heart, reminding me that God always has plans for our good and never for woe. His plans always prosper not just me but my family, and he had the same good plans for this precious little girl he would send us.

The incredible thing is that it turned out that this conference and the talk I heard would provide the affirmation and comfort I would need to say yes to adopting Faithy just twelve days later. We'd been in the adoption process for more than a year and hadn't yet been matched with a child, though we knew the match was getting closer. On April 28, our adoption agency sent over an adorable picture of Wu Feng Hua, a three-year-old child who was deaf. They believed she was a perfect match for us. If I hadn't heard Kerri's talk and attended the Divine Mercy Sunday conference that helped me understand God's boundless love and mercy for me, I don't think I would have had the courage to relinquish all my fears and trust completely in God's amazing plan to bring Faithy home to us.

Theory to Reality

Although the conference had strengthened my resolve to adopt an older child, there was still a part of me of me that desired an infant.

Perhaps I wished for a type of do-over, to learn from all my parenting mistakes and do a better job than I felt I had with my first two children. However, two days after this conference, again in prayer, the Lord reminded me gently of my not-so-fondness for infant care—being spit up on, changing diapers, and waking for midnight feedings. Interestingly, I would later learn that my then ten-year-old son, Ian, had been praying for a preschool sibling because he didn't want the age between him and his new sister to be so vast that they wouldn't know each other. This process taught me that sometimes God has other prayers than mine to answer. God used this adoption to teach me quite a lot.

When my phone rang at three o'clock, the holy hour of mercy, on April 28—God's perfect timing if you ask me—I was prepared with abundant graces to move ahead on this mission from God. On the other end of the line, Meg from CAWLI asked, "How serious are you about adopting a deaf child?" My heart did a double handspring layout. *How serious? Are you kidding!* I knew instantly that this was finally her! Our daughter was finally being born into our hearts. God had prepared me my whole life through my love of ASL, Deaf culture, and the idea of adoption, and here it was coming to fruition. He indeed did have amazing plans for me. Then Meg from the adoption agency added what I had been prepared to hear, "There is just one thing," she said, "She's not an infant as we had discussed. She's actually three, nearly four years old." I think I laughed out loud and said, "It's okay, I was actually expecting that."

She said to take twenty-four hours to make our decision, then added, "Do you want me to send her picture over?" Typically, they would not do that, so you could decide without being coerced by the cute face. But I insisted on the cute face; I knew it was the last clue I needed to be affirmed in our decision. As soon as I opened the attachment and saw her little face, I knew without a shadow of a doubt this was my daughter. She even resembled my younger son, Adam, who looks just like me. Only God could make a 100 percent Chinese little girl resemble a half Portuguese and half French-Canadian little boy.

What I didn't know at that point, however, is that the six- to eight-week wait we had been promised would become a six-month wait. The Lord teaches us so many things, answers so many questions, and brings so many consolations. Although I wanted her with me immediately, in hindsight I see his perfect plan in all of this. Again, during that six-month period, I was not the only one whose prayers he was answering. It was a painful wait, don't get me wrong, but in that time, my devotion to the Divine Mercy and to introducing it to my family became more powerful; it was how I navigated every delay we received and kept my heart at peace. It was how I kept myself from fearing that this little girl who I had fallen madly in love with at first sight would not come home to us. And it was this devotion that the Lord used to comfort me in my fear that I was inadequate to be this little girl's mom. Through this journey and this beautiful devotion, I learned that God's will and Jesus's love for us, are both truly love and mercy itself.

Consolation and a Sense of Humor

In September 2009, with more than a month left before we could travel to China and bring Faithy home, I decided to distract myself by spending the evening enjoying dinner with a friend, who also happened to be a special education teacher. I disclosed to my friend my plans to homeschool my daughter along with her two brothers. I wished to keep her home, at least for a little while, to get her acclimated to and experienced with family life. My wise and kind friend understood that the intricacies of teaching a child with hearing loss required a special skill that, although I was well trained in early childhood education, I did not possess. Gently, she explained the importance for me of being open to investigating options for schools that served deaf and hard of hearing students.

Overwrought from contemplating what I could not provide for my daughter instead of all the wonderful things I could offer her, I went home weighted beneath my escalating doubts and insecurities. I sat in her prepared but empty bedroom and cried. I told the Lord I was the wrong person for this mission. "I can't do any of this," I sobbed, and went to find my Bible for consolation. Realizing my Bible was in the room with my sleeping husband, I instead picked up St. Faustina's *Diary*, purchased after the novena piqued my interest in Faustina and her encounters with Christ, which I had left on the coffee table. I opened to these words:

> [Jesus] said, **My daughter, why are you giving in to thoughts of fear?** I answered, "O Lord, You know why."

And He said, **Why?** "This work frightens me. You know
that I am incapable of carrying it out." And He said, **Why?**
"You see very well that I am not in good health, that I have
no education, that I have no money, that I am an abyss
of misery, that I fear contacts with people. Jesus, I desire
only You. You can release me from this." And the Lord
said to me, **My daughter, what you have said is true. You
are very miserable, and it pleased Me to carry out this
work of mercy precisely through you who are nothing
but misery itself. Do not fear; I will not leave you alone.
Do whatever you can in this matter; I will accomplish
everything that is lacking in you. You know what is within your power to do; do that.** The Lord looked into the
depth of my being with great kindness; I thought I would
die for joy under that gaze. The Lord disappeared, and joy,
(253) strength and power to act remained in my soul. But I
was surprised that the Lord did not want to release me and
that He is not changing anything He has once said. And
despite all these joys, there is always a shadow of sorrow. I
see that love and sorrow go hand in hand. (881)

I burst into that intense place between hysterical laughter and
uncontrollable tears. I shared each worry of Faustina's, except for me
it was regarding my vocation to be Faithy's mother. I lacked the proper
education to be the best teacher for her, we had no money to complete
the adoption, and my anxiety threatened to keep me from even flying
to bring her home. I was indeed misery itself.

Jesus did not sugarcoat his response to Faustina—or to me as I
poured my heart on Faithy's bedroom floor that night. "**My daughter,
what you have said is true. You are very miserable**" (*Diary*, 881).
As difficult (and humorous) as those words were to hear, the next
brought such a rush of relief, I could barely breathe as I read them.
"**Do whatever you can in this matter; I will accomplish everything
that is lacking in you. You know what is within your power to do;
do that**" (*Diary*, 881). How many circumstances do we find ourselves
in, thinking, *I cannot do this, I lack everything to accomplish it*? What
comfort I took, and I pray you do as well, in knowing, "You are right;
you cannot do it, but God can." Nothing is impossible for him who
created day and night, told the stars where to go, and decided how far

the ocean could come onto the land. Do what you can, and know that he is faithful and will do the rest.

I continued to pray at three o'clock each day, asking for peace in the waiting and for safe travels. We were blessed with both. As for educating my daughter, I did stay open to what was best for her. Faithy remained at home with her brothers and me for five years. When she was adjusted and my education skills were at their limit, we found her the most amazing school for the Deaf that she adores. She even shares her forty-five–minute van ride with another little girl her same age, also named Faith.

Prayer in the Three O'Clock Hour

While the agony of waiting for my child to arrive paled in comparison with Jesus's suffering for the sins of the world, my heart found comfort in knowing that my prayers during this holiest hour had extra merit. St. Faustina recorded the words of Jesus regarding the three o'clock hour in her diary:

> **I remind you, My daughter, that as often as you hear the clock strike the third hour, immerse yourself completely in My mercy, adoring and glorifying it; invoke its omnipotence for the whole world, and particularly for poor sinners; for at that moment mercy was opened wide for every soul. In this hour you can obtain everything for yourself and for others for the asking; it was the hour of grace for the whole world — mercy triumphed over justice.** (*Diary*, 1572)

I set my watch alarm to sound each day at three o'clock. More than ten years later, that alarm is still set. Some days I have time to recite an entire chaplet; other days, I have just a minute to thank Jesus for his salvific work upon the cross. Always, I ask him to bless my day and to help me to grow in trust, hope, and faith.

The answers are always in accordance with the Father's will, and not mine—hence the great need for trust in our lives. I know I struggle with my desire to avoid suffering, to have only the good I pray for in my life, and have to work at remembering that all that God allows is for my good. He knows the big-picture reason for the suffering, and if he did not spare his only Son suffering, we can believe in the ultimate good brought about from our own suffering.

Maybe We Should Name Her Patience

On September 24, 2009, instead of being on an airplane heading for China, I was sitting at home, lamenting yet another delay, trying not to lose hope. Since April, I had prayed the Divine Mercy Chaplet diligently every day at three o'clock, clinging to the promises Jesus shared with St. Faustina about that precious hour—the hour when Jesus gave up his life for the remission of our sins, a sacred moment he implored each of us to mark, even for a moment, every day. The words from St. Faustina's *Diary* that I particularly clung to were these: "**In this hour, I will refuse nothing to the soul that makes a request of Me in virtue of My Passion**" (*Diary*, 1320).

Leading up to that day, I thought I'd seen every sign and had every affirmation that we would truly be going at last. Even the *Magnificat* prayer for the day included Hebrews 11:1 ("Now faith is the assurance of things hoped for, the conviction of things not seen"), the very first verse I took her name from. But it was not to be. We received word that it would be at least three more weeks before we could go to China and bring Faithy home. Here's the caveat, if you will, about that promise from Jesus: what is given always has to be in perfect alignment with God's will for you. As a loving Father, he will withhold even good things if they will not benefit his ultimate goal for us to be with him in heaven forever.

As a mother, there are many times I have delayed responding to a child's request for the child's own good. For instance, bedtime requests for candy would not be granted. Candy in itself is not evil, but there is a time and place when it is best consumed. Additionally, whether they liked the lesson or not, my response was to help them build the necessary virtues of patience, temperance, and prudence. I didn't like waiting nearly seven months to finally meet my little girl; however, with the gift of hindsight, I can be grateful for the faith strengthened and virtues honed—especially patience—and the many other prayers answered along the way.

As I sat in prayer, the Lord revealed to my heart the question of where he is more glorified: in the one who gets all he asked for or in the one who has to wait and maybe even doesn't get what he wants, and yet still loves God. I prayed that it's not in the one who gets nothing and still loves him, of course, and I prayed that was not his plan for us. Yet I was hopeful and still believed he would fulfill all that he had said, that he would bring to completion the good work he had started. I noted in my journal that morning that I was hoping on his mercy, that he would do as he intended to do and had told us and would provide us soon with travel so that we could teach her all about our beautiful faith and so that she could know him. That had surprisingly been something I hadn't thought about at the beginning of the process—that I wasn't just adding to our family, but that we would be adding this beautiful little girl to his family through baptism.

How amazing it would be, I thought that morning, to teach her the prayers and about his great love for her. To show her our beautiful New England autumns; to celebrate her first Christmas, with the lights of the shrine nearby; to drive around in awe of the Christmas lights on people's homes—I doubted it she had ever seen anything like it. To show her her Tinkerbell room with the adorable clothes I had lovingly picked out for her. To cuddle with her during our cold New England nights. I longed to dress her for the first snow—coming from a place affectionately known as a furnace city, she would find this very new. To watch her discover the world with words formed on her hands and never said before because no one had taught her yet how to communicate. Until then, I'd been afraid to ponder life with a daughter. Even as I wrote the words, I was afraid to wish too hard or imagine too much. "Please, Lord," I begged that day, "I pray, let this be your plan for us."

I ended that prayer time with this phrase attributed to Padre Pio: "Pray, hope, don't worry, worry is useless! God hears our prayers, and he answers them."[1] And in just two short months, answer them he would!

Faithy's First Confession

Divine Mercy has continued to come through for our family over the years. In April, 2015, Faithy was ready to make her first Communion and, of course, her first Confession, I worried about how to make this happen for her in the most natural way. I am allowed to interpret for her in the confessional, and it is not as though at the age of eight, with a mild cognitive disability, she'd have any sins that she'd be embarrassed to share in front of her mother; however, there is still always a desire for her to encounter life's milestones just as everyone else does. I prayed and beseeched St. Faustina's intercession, especially during my daily three o'clock Divine Mercy Chaplet. Shortly, after seeking the Spirit's guidance in Faithy's first confession, I learned that the Boston Deaf Apostolate, led by Fr. Shawn Carey, a priest who is also deaf, was offering sacramental prep for first Communion. I contacted the office, and by a grace only God could give, they had a first Communion retreat scheduled for Divine Mercy Sunday!

Faithy and I attended, and it was a beautiful experience from the opening prayer to the moment she entered the confessional on her own to receive the sacrament from Fr. Shawn, who could lead her through it in her native language! Acting in persona Christi, he provided in the generosity of his vocation and through the amazing grace of God this natural, merciful encounter with Christ. Oh, and did I mention she walked through the doors of the confessional at precisely three o'clock? That was divine mercy, indeed!

St. Faustina

St. Maria Faustina Kowalska was born on August 25, 1905, in Głogowiec, Poland, to a poor but religious family. Faustina, baptized and known in her family as Helena (Helen), was the third of ten children. At the age of seven, she had already felt the first stirrings of a religious vocation. She made her first Holy Communion at the age of nine, the moment she corresponds to her first awareness of the presence of the Divine Guest, Jesus, within her soul. She attended school for only three years. After finishing school, she wanted to enter the convent, but her parents would not give her permission. At sixteen, Helen left home and went to work as a housekeeper in Aleksandrów, Łódź, and Ostrówek to support herself and help her parents.

Faustina entered the Congregation of the Sisters of Our Lady of Mercy on August 1, 1925, and took the name Sr. Maria Faustina of the Most Blessed Sacrament. In her diary she records that the

Lord Jesus, addressing her as "**Secretary of My most profound mystery**," told her, "**Your task is to write down everything that I make known to you about My mercy, for the benefit of those who by reading these things will be comforted in their souls and will have the courage to approach Me**" (*Diary*, 1693).

Her recording of her countless conversations and encounters with Jesus and Mary would lead her to become known as the patron saint of mercy. What one learns after any amount of time with Faustina's *Diary* is her great devotion to Adoration of the Blessed Sacrament. In its pages you will find countless inspiring prayers written by Faustina, some of the most poignant and powerful written for time in adoration of the Lord. In the final hours of 1934, Sr. Faustina was permitted to stay awake and spend the entire evening in Adoration before Christ in the Eucharist. As the clock struck midnight, she broke out into a litany of praise to Jesus in the Eucharist: "O Blessed Host!" She would conclude with "I do not understand how it is possible not to trust in Him who can do all things. With Him, everything; without Him, nothing. He is Lord. He will not allow those who have placed all their trust in Him to be put to shame" (*Diary*, 355–358).

The Vatican biography of this great saint offers this conclusion to the account of her life: "Sister Mary Faustina, consumed by tuberculosis and by innumerable sufferings which she accepted as a voluntary sacrifice for sinners, died in Krakow at the age of just thirty-three on October 5, 1938 with a reputation for spiritual maturity and a mystical union with God."[2]

The Divine Mercy Devotion

> I realize more and more how much every soul needs God's mercy throughout life and particularly at the hour of death. This chaplet [of Divine Mercy] mitigates God's anger, as He Himself told me.
>
> —*St. Faustina*

The Divine Mercy devotion consists of several parts—the image, the feast, the Hour of Great Mercy (three o'clock), the chaplet, and the novena.

The Divine Mercy image (actually there are two) was commissioned from the visions of Jesus experienced by St. Faustina and includes the words "Jesus, I Trust in You" along the bottom. During the revelations to St. Faustina in the 1930s, Our Lord called for a special feast day to be celebrated on the Sunday after Easter. That day, now known as Divine Mercy Sunday, was named by Pope St. John Paul II at the canonization of St. Faustina on April 30, 2000; and in a move only the Holy Spirit could orchestrate, it would also be the feast day upon which he died just five years later on April 2, 2005.

The Divine Mercy Novena of Chaplets can be prayed anytime and comes with Jesus's promise: "**By this novena** [of chaplets]**, I will grant every possible grace to souls**" (*Diary*, 796). However, it has become a tradition to begin the novena on Good Friday to conclude on Divine Mercy Sunday. The words of the novena and how to pray the chaplet itself can be found on the website for the Marian Fathers (TheDivineMercy.org).

Adopting a More Tangible Faith

Growing in Grace with Scripture

> Do not despise prophesying, but test everything; hold fast what is good, abstain from every form of evil. May the God of peace himself sanctify you wholly; and may your spirit and soul and body be kept sound and blameless at the coming of our Lord Jesus Christ. He who calls you is faithful, and he will do it. (1 Thes 5:20–24)

How much are you trying to accomplish? How much are you allowing Christ to accomplish for you? What steals your peace? Do you worry about what might be, what could be, or what may never be? What is your response to the grace God provides to help you discern what is good, what is necessary, and what can be left behind? Our cooperation with grace—with his Holy Spirit working within us, animating our movements toward holiness—is what makes being an adopted son or daughter so magnificent. Those things we think are impossible, God tells us are possible because of his grace. Everything, as St. Thérèse says, is grace.

Test everything; retain what is good, and that includes advice. Do not test it against the world but with the Word, in prayer, with a trusted friend who is faithful not just to you but to the Lord as well.

As we discerned the adoption, my reliance on sacramental devotions—including my time in the prayers associated with each that united my prayers with those of the Church—prepared my heart to receive all the grace I needed to say yes to this mission for God.

Every day when I prayed that Divine Mercy Novena, especially with my little boys as we waited out God's plan, we found peace and comfort. It was how we prayed constantly, rejoiced in every circumstance, and continued to thank God for what he was doing in our lives and with our family. It helped us maintain peace in the months of waiting, and it helped us to make many difficult decisions along the way, such as whether to travel alone and take our chances that the Chinese government would allow us in to complete the adoption, or whether to wait another month and travel with other families. My heart, so eager to meet Faithy, wanted to take the chance, but the more I prayed, the more I brought my petitions to God in that three o'clock hour, the more I realized that his plan for us was to wait. It was, in the end, the perfect plan; we made many amazing friends, and we didn't have to worry about whether we would be able to complete the adoption process.

Prayer pours out graces, an unexplained strength which at times feels almost tangible, and during this long nine months' wait, kept me hopeful that the promise of being this little girl's mother would be fulfilled in his perfect time. The words "Blessed is she who believed that there would be a fulfilment of what was spoken to her from the Lord" (Lk 1:45) that gushed forth from Elizabeth to the Blessed Virgin Mary became a model of hope. These words led me to a greater trust in God's plan for my life—offering a more profound meaning to "Jesus, I trust in you." God is faithful, and he fulfills his promises—maybe not on my timeline, but he is trustworthy. St. Faustina, the Blessed Mother, the beautiful Divine Mercy Chaplet, and our understanding of the devotion of Divine Mercy helped our family navigate that difficult waiting time.

Uncovering Grace

1. Does your family have a prayer you turn to in difficult times that helps you navigate through them? Do you pray this together? If not, what obstacles do you believe keep you from family prayer?
2. Can you recall a time when a prayer was answered in the most unusual or unexpected way? What emotions does this memory evoke? What is something about how God answers your prayers that always amazes you?
3. Do you see God, especially in the person of Jesus, as trustworthy? What circumstances have helped you formulate this opinion of God? How can Jesus's promises from the Hour of Great Mercy restore peace to your heart and affirm that he can indeed be trusted with your every care?

Grace-Building Activities

- Set an alarm on your watch, your smart home device, or even your fitness tracker to chime every day at three o'clock. Even for just a moment at that time, remember Jesus's Passion and say a prayer of thanksgiving, just as he told St. Faustina to: "**At three o'clock, implore My mercy, especially for sinners; and, if only for a brief moment, immerse yourself in My Passion, particularly in My abandonment at the moment of agony. This is the hour of great mercy for the whole world**" (*Diary*, 1320). When time allows, pray the Divine Mercy Chaplet or, if able, make the Stations of the Cross.
- When praying the Divine Mercy Chaplet, call to mind someone who has passed away for every bead of the chaplet. If praying it with others, take turns naming a person or an intention. Maybe you can even try singing it, as is often done; you can find several variations on YouTube. Consider gathering a group together on First Fridays, especially at three o'clock, to pray the chaplet together.

- Create a beautiful visual to help you and your family remember to pray the Divine Mercy Novena of Chaplets. You might do this starting on Good Friday and leading up to Divine Mercy Sunday. The visual is based on the words of the chaplet given to Faustina by Jesus: **"O Blood and Water which gushed forth from the Heart of Jesus as a Fount of Mercy for us, I trust in You!"** (*Diary*, 309). Begin by creating a banner that reads, "Jesus, I Trust in You" (its size and degree of ornateness are up to you and your family's aesthetics); this goes up on the first day of the novena. Then make four red streamers and four blue ones. The red represents the blood that came from Jesus's heart, and the blue the water as depicted in the Divine Mercy image. You can use crepe paper, construction paper folded accordion-style to mimic a cascading effect, or plain paper. Attach one streamer on each of the remaining days of the novena. You may wish to write a few words on each streamer to help you remember the intention for each day.

3

Surrendering to the Cross

St. Padre Pio, Relics, and Crucifixes

If we only try to show the Dear Lord a good will and ask Him for resignation to the crosses he sends or permits to come our way, we may be sure that sooner or later they will turn out to have been just so many blessings in disguise.

—*Bl. Solanus Casey*

Blessings in the Waiting

Waiting is not my superpower. I learned long ago in my spiritual journey never to pray for patience when I discovered it is not instantly infused but usually comes through circumstances that require you to practice the virtue. Whether I wanted to participate or not, the long wait between April 2009, and traveling to China in November 2009, required an outpouring of grace and growth in many virtues. Thanks be to God, I decided to lean into the grace and those nine months became a time for finding comfort in the waiting, feeling like I was doing something each day to help shorten our wait to bring Faithy home, even if that something was finding the peace that comes in prayer.

I also kept myself busy by seeking solid spiritual events to pass the time positively and productively. One event, which fell on September 28, the exact date of our initially planned but subsequently canceled trip to China, would prove particularly advantageous. It was a retreat day at an abbey in the most idyllic New England autumn location. Listening to an inspiring speaker and participating in the recitation of the Rosary and the Divine Mercy Chaplet, among other spirit-filled elements, were just the respite I needed from all the adoption woes.

One surprise from the day—venerating a bloody glove (kept in a protective bag, in case you are curious about the logistics) worn by stigmatist and mystic Padre Pio—would be life changing and lead me to a close relationship with this incredible saint. Padre Pio had the rare charism of bearing the stigmata, the wounds of Christ: nail marks in his hands and feet, and a wound from the spear in his side.

Padre Pio and I shared the world for only three short months, his passing coming in the year I was born. I found this fascinating because until that day, I had thought of saints as people who lived long, long before me. I'd never heard of Padre Pio, his spiritual fatherhood, and his desire not to enter heaven until he'd brought all his beloved *children* along with him. Known as his great promise, Padre Pio stated many times, "I will ask the Lord to let me remain at the threshold of Paradise, and I will not enter until the last of my spiritual children has entered."[1] This experience would also be my first time encountering the veneration of a relic, a show of respect (not worship) through reverently touching the sacred treasure (a body part of a saint, such as bone, blood, or flesh) with a kiss, one's hand, or other holy objects.

A carefully preserved glove that Padre Pio had worn to cover his stigmata on his hands was delicately removed from a velvet-lined box. With all the piety I could muster, I prayerfully approached the glove and touched all the sacramentals dangling from my necklace—a crucifix, a Miraculous Medal, and a metal scapular—to the glove. Like sacramentals, relics are not magic, and grace bestowed by God through them depends solely on the disposition of the one praying with that sacramental and, of course, on God's will.

Supercharging Sacramentals

My research into this new man in my life first brought me to one of his most famous quotes and enlightened me as to why the Holy Spirit might have brought me to him: "Pray, hope, don't worry. Worry is useless. God is merciful and will hear your prayer." I am a worrier. If you could medal in emotion, I'd be a gold medalist in anxiety! My crucifix had long been a place I found solace and comfort, reaching for it to remind myself that Jesus is never far from me. I am surprised that after nearly twenty years, the corpus remains visible and hasn't been worn off! Realizing that now when I placed this tiny cross between my fingers, I had extra prayer support through Padre Pio, opened a new door of seeking out other relics to touch and bless my sacramentals.

Over the years since, I've been blessed to attend special events and services involving the relics of St. Charbel Makhlouf, St. Maria Goretti, St. John Vianney, Padre Pio again (his heart), and Pope St. John Paul II, and even to visit an exposition of more than one hundred relics brought by Fr. Carlos Martins. I've also visited the shrines and graves of St. Katharine Drexel, St. Gianna Molla, St. Thérèse of Lisieux, St. Elizabeth Ann Seton, Ven. Patrick Peyton, and Bl. Stanley Rother, among others. I am a big fan of "holy field trips."

Sharing the Passion of Christ in ASL

In the introduction, I shared my initial concerns about how to teach the faith to my daughter. Through pictures, books, stained glass windows, cartoon videos, and various sacramentals, we managed reasonably well. The crucifix, however, required something more than just holding it up for her to gaze upon; without the story of the Passion, I knew she'd never fully grasp the power of this image.

Over time, the Spirit would open the pathway to bridging the gap between what she saw and the depth of what she was seeing. In September of 2014, Faithy began attending the Learning Center for the Deaf and became my teacher of her beautiful language. Both of our abilities with ASL flourished, providing new opportunities for me to share the Word of God with her. The first Palm Sunday I felt confident enough to interpret the entire reading of the Passion will always stand out not only as a memory of a parenting win but also as a time when the Lord taught me.

My children are known to refer to Palm Sunday as "that day in church that requires us to stand forever and ever (amen)." It is the service that turns most of our children into spaghetti-legged, blob-o-kids. That first Palm Sunday after I had returned to regularly attending Church, my own adult body balked when I heard the priest announce, "This morning we'll be following the *long* form of the Gospel."

At first, I felt that pang of impending exhaustion as I realized that not only would I be standing for "all that time," but even more important, I would be translating for "all that time." Since I am passionate about the Passion, however, my overwhelmed feeling was quickly replaced with the excitement of being allowed to share some of scripture's most poignant verses through one of the most beautifully expressive languages.

In keeping with the shower of God's graces on our family throughout our journey, the ASL glossing (interpreting) guidelines, *Signing the Scriptures* by Joan Blake, mysteriously showed up in my mailbox. The fascinating thing for me was not so much the mechanics of ASL these manuals offered but this entirely new, thought-provoking, and visually rich way of looking at God's Word.

St. Matthew's Passion account begins with Judas betraying Jesus for only thirty pieces of silver. After Judas is paid the money, the next part of the scene, "And from that moment he sought an opportunity to betray him" (Mt 26:16), is signed, "Now he wait, jump-at-chance." The use of that particular phrase struck me because it brings to mind a positive opportunity.

Poor Judas, my heart is always so heavy for him during the Holy Week readings. He was so misguided; there must have been something good in him for Jesus to have selected him as a disciple. I tend to side with the scripture scholars who believe Judas truly felt in his heart that he was doing Jesus a favor by handing him over to the chief priest. What if Judas's motives were to help Jesus "jump-at-chance" to launch his long-awaited kingdom? The irony, of course, is that Judas does help Jesus to do that, but not in any way he probably ever imagined.

Next comes the preparation for the Passover meal. The disciples (signed as "followers") wonder where to cook the dinner. While working through how to interpret this portion of the story, so that Faithy would best understand, I was moved by one phrase from scripture not suggested in the *Signing the Scriptures* book. Jesus instructs the disciples with these words: "Go into the city to a certain man and tell him, 'The teacher says, "My appointed time draws near . . ."'" (Mt 26:18, *Lectionary for Mass*). Those five little words, "My appointed time draws near," are serious game-changers. Sometimes the words suggested in the ASL translation guide give me pause, and sometimes it is the pieces left out. I can attest to the sometimes-difficult task of expressing all the profound beauty, emotion, and message of the Gospels in ASL when interpreting, especially if someone reads the Word too quickly.

Now comes the Last Supper (see Matthew 26:17–29). I love interpreting this event each week during the liturgy; this section of the consecration is so visual and gestural. As signer, you take on the position of Jesus at the table, the bread and wine before you. Your eyes look to the heavens as you give God thanks and praise. You mime taking the bread into your hands and breaking it. You give a piece to each of the disciples, one by one, and sign, "Take, eat, this my body." Then you sign "Finish" and take up the cup. Again, you look to the heavens and emphasize how Jesus gave God thanks and praise. You offer the cup to the disciples, followed by "Drink this, all, this my blood, means new promise-connect. Blood I lose for many, their sins forgive." It is hard not to lose yourself in the moment and feel you are at the table with Jesus (blessed to be at his vantage point)—witnessing the institution of the Eucharist.

They sing a hymn (a detail I had always missed when listening to the Passion) and go to the Mount of Olives. Jesus shares how their faith, that very night, will be shaken. "Peter tell-him, 'Maybe they doubt, but I doubt never'" (Mt 26:33). Ah, how boldly Peter proclaims those words, and in his heart, I am sure he believed he would be strong enough to fulfill them. How many times do I, like Peter, proclaim those exact words about my faith but, likewise in weakness or fear, fall into doubt or deny with some word or action.

In the garden, Jesus says, "My Father, if it is possible, let this cup pass from me; yet, not as I will, but as you will" (Mt 26:39, *Lectionary*). This line is one of the most challenging for me to interpret because of my own struggle to live these words. In ASL, your facial expression is as vital to the meaning and tone of the sentence as what your hands are doing. As I read the ASL phrases, I am to string together: "Father, suffer die, I don't want, but your will I accept." The starkness of Jesus's agony, portrayed in bare-bones wording, cuts like the soldier's sword as my hands and expressions work to correctly convey Jesus's poignant, painful submission to the Father's perfect will.

Judas arrives and betrays the Master with a kiss. Jesus replies, "Friend, do what you have come for" (Mt 26:50, *Lectionary*). The use of the word *friend* is so profound. It seems so out of place in the dark, ominous setting. "Friend" is one of the first signs we teach children. It is the sign I utilize to help my daughter understand who is safe to approach or be with, often explaining to her that the new person standing before her is "Mommy's friend." It gives me comfort that she can identify friend from foe—though our eyes can be deceiving. Judas, in the eyes of the world, is now a foe, but he is still a friend in the eyes of Jesus.

After hearing of Peter's denial and Judas's demise, we are introduced to Pontius Pilate and Barabbas. I absolutely love the ASL description of Barabbas: "one prisoner awful." That sums him up nicely.

Pilate will not take responsibility for the Crucifixion and symbolically washes his hands of the situation. English idioms are typically not used in ASL; many just do not translate. For example, it could be confusing and even perhaps a little frightening to sign "It is raining cats and dogs" to describe the weather outside. Besides being messy and dangerous, and let's not forget impossible, it is also clearly not the intended meaning. That principle applies here: instead of hand washing, the ASL phrase "hands-off" is chosen to express Pilate's stance. The sign is created by making a "disgusted" facial expression, head turned slightly away, tight-lipped, nose turned up, and your fingers brush off the top of your shoulders, denoting you are not a part of, not involved in, or not responsible for anything that is about to happen. Now that, I believe, sums up Pilate's stance on the situation. Coward.

St. Matthew then makes relatively quick work of moving the Gospel from the moment Jesus is condemned to death to his time on the Cross—though I am sure most eight- or ten-year-olds who have stood for the entire reading would argue strongly against my perception of the time concept of "quick work." Now, if that eight-year-old has been at Mass with us, they at least have something to occupy their eyes as well as their ears.

While I am happy to have people admiring the beauty of ASL, it is difficult during the consecration to have the focus shifted away from the most profound moment and mystery any of us will ever witness on earth to my interpreting. In the end, however, it is about providing access to language for my daughter, and I pray that if people find themselves watching, they may be listening even closer and, by the grace of God, will find a new way to view the Word of God. Amen.

The True Cross and Miracles

One of the great Triduum traditions in my little country parish is attaching a relic of the True Cross to the giant wooden cross we venerate on Good Friday. Both Kevin and I believed that the validity of this relic as from the True Cross was determined by a deaf woman's miraculous regaining of her hearing. So, every year after Faithy returned to the pew after venerating the cross, unbeknownst to the other, Kevin and I would each lean over and whisper in her ear to ask if she could hear us—just checking if God had willed for another such miracle from this relic.

For years, every Good Friday, we both secretly hoped this would be the year she'd receive a miracle of hearing. Now that she's older, I decided to share what had been happened behind the scenes, so to speak, for the past ten years. In her usual unassuming, sweet way, she laughed but quickly reminded me she's happy deaf. It is how God made her, she said, and she's fine with that. In fact, she teased, "I never get awoken during middle of the night thunderstorms like you do, Mom!" Faithy approaches almost everything in an innocent, joy-filled way; to her nothing feels like a cross; she trusts God's will so purely, it never ceases to impress me! I'm okay with how God made her too, but that doesn't mean I'm going to stop bringing her to venerate that relic every Good Friday and leaning over to whisper in her ear—just to check. Even if I did recently learn while sharing this chapter with my spiritual director (the pastor who had shared the story) that the miracle associated with the validity of the True Cross relic was the healing of a woman on her *death* bed, not the healing of a *deaf* woman! Although Faithy's hearing has not been restored, our family did receive an enormous grace in the experience of venerating the cross together every Good Friday; one could even say we received a healing, albeit a spiritual rather than a physical one.

Witnessing to Faithy stories of the many ways God moves in our lives through sacramentals, such as the cross I wear which touched Padre Pio's relic which blessed it, brings us closer and are all ways to pass along a tangible faith to her. Plus, stories surrounding the sacramentals I share with her are incredibly entertaining to retell in ASL! There is a reason Jesus used stories (parables) to teach and share the faith: we are drawn to story. We can relate, and it engages us. I may not like the cross and may find it difficult to embrace it with a good ol' "Lord, let thy will be done," but in the end, it is his perfect will that I accept, and that typically comes with a fantastic story (or two)!

My Padre Pio Pilot Intercession

Travel isn't always easy for me. During a business trip to Philadelphia, my flight home was canceled due to severe weather. I stayed remarkably calm despite the airline rescheduling my return flight for two days later. I took a deep breath and prayed for help from Padre Pio. Why him?

Years before, I had read testimony of American pilots who converted to Catholicism after a "ghost" monk appeared in the sky before them during bombing missions over Italy in World War II. They reported that the monk's hands were raised, forbidding bombs to be dropped on his beloved town and monastery, and according to the pilots, the planes were turned around away from their intended targets, without any help from them. The town was San Giovanni Rotondo, home to Padre Pio's Capuchin monastery.[2] I knew if anyone could help me solve pilot issues, it would be him. I finished my prayer, took another deep breath, and began my search for a way home.

I quickly dismissed taking a bus when I realized it arrived in a sketchy location nearly an hour from my home at three in the morning. The next option was a train departing in less than an hour, but this left me too little time to locate my luggage and secure transportation to the train station. Since I was only six hours from home, a car seemed the most logical choice.

At baggage claim, I saw a young woman I'd had a brief chat with earlier in the day and invited her to rent a car with me to get back to

Massachusetts. However, she had to phone her parents to make sure they were okay with this plan. I chuckled when I heard overheard her say, "No, Dad, it is fine. I'm pretty sure she's safe because she's an older woman." Apparently, they agreed I fit the "safe criteria" because they allowed her to come home with me.

We headed over to the only rental agency offering one-way car rentals. In front of us in line was a pilot from the same airline we had been scheduled to fly on. Not being shy, I struck up a conversation with him, asking if he was our pilot from the canceled flight. He explained that he was finishing up his shift for the weekend, and he had only used that flight to get back home. "Oddly," he said, "I was supposed to be on an earlier one, but something kept me from taking it."

He was called to the counter, where the woman begrudgingly gave him what turned out to be the last one-way rental to Boston, most likely because he had on his pilot uniform. The kind pilot, knowing from our conversation how eager I was to get home to see my god-son off to Marine boot camp the next day, offered to take the young woman and me home if we wanted. The ride was amazing; the three of us had much in common and chatted nonstop for six hours. I was so engaged with my new friends that I forgot to tell my husband I'd found a way home.

My phone beeped with an eager text asking me where I was and what was happening. "Do I need to get in the car and head to Phila-delphia?" my husband sweetly inquired. "Nope," I replied, "I am fine, and hitching a ride back with a pilot." Confused, he responded, "You rented a Honda Pilot?" "No, silly, I'm being driven home by an actual *pilot*"—and *godcidentally* one from the very airline I was supposed to fly that day!

Padre Pio

Francesco Forgione, later known to the world as Padre Pio, entered the world on May 25, 1887, in Pietrelcina, Italy. Francesco nurtured his love for the Blessed Virgin Mary from childhood, praying to "Our Lady of Graces" and offering the Efficacious Novena to the Sacred Heart of Jesus (more about this powerful novena included in chapter 10) every day for all those who asked for prayers. At the age of fifteen, he took the habit of the Order of Friars Minor Capuchin on January 22, 1903, and assumed the name of Pio in honor of St. Pius V, the patron saint of Pietrelcina. A humble and holy priest, he is known for his extraordinary spiritual life, including the gifts of healing, bilocation, prophecy, miracles, discernment of spirits, the ability to read hearts, and the gift of tongues.

His life and ministry were so filled with abundant graces as well as great suffering, especially from the wounds of the stigmata that he carried for fifty years, that even his superiors at one point requested he refrain from public ministry due to the hysteria from the faithful seeking his prayers and soul reading confessions was creating around him. Padre Pio died on September 23, 1968, in San Giovanni Rotondo, Italy.

In addition to his spiritual generosity, Padre Pio also had a great sense of humor: it is recorded that when people asked if they could become his spiritual child, he would respond, "Yes, but don't make me look bad."[3] Many years ago, after learning we could still ask that question of him, I did so, and although sometimes I fail at keeping my half of the bargain, I know he indeed loves and cares for me as one of his own. My father shared Padre Pio's May 25 birthday. And while my father and I did eventually reconcile our relationship, he would never be a devout Catholic, so I always found it comforting to know I had a spiritual father to guide, reassure, and pray for me.

Veneration of the Cross

Proclaim your fiat too, as much in propitious times as in adverse circumstances. Do not worry or wrestle with how you will be able to express it. We know that human nature avoids difficult things, like the cross, but that does not mean the soul is not submitted to God's will once it is understood.

—*Padre Pio*

During the seventh century, the Roman Church adopted the practice of Veneration of the Cross from the Church in Jerusalem, where a fragment of wood that is believed to be from the Lord's Cross had been venerated every year on Good Friday since the fourth century.[4] According to tradition, a part of the Holy Cross was discovered by St. Helena, mother of the Roman emperor Constantine, on a pilgrimage to Jerusalem in 326 and brought back to Rome. A coffer of gold-plated silver that contained the wood of the Cross was brought forward. The bishop placed the relic on a table in the Chapel of the Crucifixion[5] in Jerusalem and the faithful went closer to it, touching brow, eyes, and lips to the wood as the priest said, "Behold, the Wood of the Cross." You probably recognize those words from current Holy Friday services as a cross is processed in for veneration by the faithful. Most churches are not blessed, as is mine, with a relic of the True Cross, so the congregation venerates the cross by either kissing or touching any part of the wood.

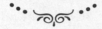

Adopting a More Tangible Faith

Growing in Grace with Scripture

> Then he said to all, "If anyone wishes to come after me, he must deny himself and take up his cross daily and follow me. For whoever wishes to save his life will lose it, but whoever loses his life for my sake will save it. What profit is there for one to gain the whole world yet lose or forfeit himself? Whoever is ashamed of me and of my words, the Son of Man will be ashamed of when he comes in his glory and in the glory of the Father and of the holy angels. Truly I say to you, there are some standing here who will not taste death until they see the kingdom of God." (Lk 9:23–27 NABRE)

Teaching the faith can be a challenge. For years, especially before adopting Faithy, I led youth retreats. One particular Confirmation retreat was exceptionally challenging, shaking my very trust in God. The retreat nearly over, I settled the students back in the main hall after a few hours in the church spent receiving the Sacrament of Reconciliation and sitting in Eucharistic Adoration. Filled with the grace from these incredible encounters with Christ, I was feeling pretty good about myself, even though corralling teens for eight hours, most against their will, had as usual created a less than friendly atmosphere. This group, despite my attempts to provide engaging activities and what I thought were interesting and lively presentations, was very difficult to reach.

It was a huge relief to glance at the clock and realize there were fewer than two hours left. "You got this," I murmured to myself and grabbed the microphone to begin my last presentation. I had barely completed the Sign of the Cross, when suddenly a young man dressed in a suit stood up.

"Excuse me," I politely addressed him, "Break is over, and we are about to pray. We are almost finished; we just have one more subject to cover." What happened next still astounds me even as I type it. "Who," he began, "do you *expletive* think you are. This has been complete *bull-expletive* you have been shoveling at us all day." Perhaps he saw an opportunity to pounce since the room had emptied of all adults except myself and the young woman whose practicum I was supervising. Before I could answer, he continued with more sentence enhancers and crazy accusations. He had clearly come with preconceived and very misguided notions of Catholicism. My presentations always focus on living the faith in our everyday lives, and I purposely steer clear of controversial subjects—because I am fully aware that apologetics are my Achilles heel. This young man perhaps sensed that as well.

The part of my brain that was presently retrieving all of my training in youth ministry and facilitating retreats was screaming "Halt, do not fall into this trap, cease all arguments now!" Oh, how I wish my brain had won. Instead, my emotions with their "I'm 100 percent in the right here" and "I can win him over" foolish pride took over, and things went from bad to absolutely horrible. The room buzzed, split between angry and uncomfortable teens. Some students stormed out (in tears). The young man continued screaming obscenities, and in fifteen short minutes, I managed to completely lose control of the retreat and destroy any good the first part of the day may have imparted. If nothing else, it was a church event the teens would never forget.

On the way home, still quite shaken, I called the young woman I was supervising to debrief the day, especially the concluding pandemonium. She wisely suggested I head to my parish, where I would find either the church or the adoration chapel open. I was grateful there was a function at our parish center, as that meant our small, private chapel would be available. I slunk into the last pew of the small chapel, put my head down on the back of the pew in front of me, and fell completely apart. "God, I am out doing your work," I sobbed, "I just want to help these kids love you. How could you do this to me!" It was the single worst moment of teaching I'd ever experienced. The more I allowed the memories of the day to wash over me, the more intense my crying became until I was just a puddle of tears, snot, and utter defeat.

Then, I felt this gentle stirring of the Holy Spirit in my heart. I raised my head and stared at the crucifix just beyond the tabernacle. In my heart I heard, *If you want to share in my glory, then you must also be willing to share in the suffering.* As these words were settling in and as the crucifix came more into focus through my tear-swollen eyes, I then heard, *If I did not spare my Son from suffering, what makes you think you'd be any different?* This profound moment of prayer concluded with my recalling the words from Luke's Gospel: "If any man would come after me, let him deny himself and take up his cross daily and follow me" (9:23).

Uncovering Grace

1. Embracing the crosses of life has to be one of Christianity's most difficult teachings. What has been your experience with surrendering to the crosses in your life? How do you personally unite your suffering with Christ's?

2. Is there a crucifix in your home? Have you ever spent time gazing upon it, contemplating the beauty that came from that moment, and offering a prayer of thanksgiving? If so, share what that was like for you; if not, consider adding this to your prayer time during the coming week.

3. Jesus taught through story, and as you've probably guessed by now, that is my favorite teaching tool as well. Can you share a story, a testimony in your life, that exemplifies a surrender and acceptance of a cross, or at least the teaching of the cross, in your life?

Grace-Building Activities

- Organize a visit to your parish, school, or diocese of the Treasures of the Church exposition (TreasuresoftheChurch.com). A ministry of evangelization of the Catholic Church run by Fr. Carlos Martins of the Companions of the Cross, as described on the website, "the exposition seeks to give people an experience of the living God through an encounter with the relics of his saints. Each exposition begins with a multimedia presentation on the Church's use of relics that is scriptural, catechetical, and devotional, leading to a renewal of the Catholic faith for many people. After the teaching, those in attendance have an opportunity to venerate the relics of some of their favorite saints." The display is breathtaking, moving, and truly something you must experience for yourself to appreciate the power of being blessed by so many holy people!

- Visit a cemetery and pray for the holy souls. You can do this anytime for a partial indulgence; however, when done during November 1 through 8 and accompanied by the reception of Holy Communion, detachment from sin, and a sacramental Confession within twenty-one days of the devotion, it confers a plenary indulgence. The grace of this indulgence may be placed upon any soul you wish. The *Catechism of the Catholic Church* explains an indulgence as "a remission before God of the temporal punishment due to sins whose guilt has already been forgiven, which the faithful Christian who is duly disposed gains under certain prescribed conditions through the action of the Church which, as the minister of redemption, dispenses and applies with authority the treasury of the satisfactions of Christ and the saints" (1471).

- Create a cross. The cross is a powerful symbol of Christian faith. During the six weeks of Lent (or any time of the year that works for you), fashion crosses to serve as a prayerful reminder of the sacrifice Jesus offered for you. Experiment with a different medium each week; for example, assemble a stained glass effect using a clear acrylic sleeve cut into a cross, framed with black construction paper, and filled with colored tissue paper. Crosses can be molded in clay, carved or whittled out of wood, drawn, even constructed from LEGO blocks. Display the crosses throughout your home as a continual reminder of Jesus's salvific work upon the True Cross more than 2,000 years ago on Good Friday.

4

A Little Prayer Never Hurts

St. Thérèse of Lisieux, Prayer Cards, and Novenas

We often think we receive graces and are divinely illuminated by means of brilliant candles. But from whence comes their light? From prayers, perhaps, of some humble, hidden soul, whose inward shining is not apparent to human eyes.

—*St. Thérèse of Lisieux*

Ask, and It Will Be Given You

As a high school junior, I was lamenting that happiness could only come if I had a boyfriend, a job, and a car. My mother suggested I pray for them. "It couldn't hurt," she added. Prayer—a novel approach—but how? I remembered a little plastic prayer card I had with a five-day prayer on it to some St. Thérèse. On day five, after I finished the prayer and began awaiting the promised rose to indicate my prayer had been heard, I headed to a friend's house. Playing badminton, I went long for a birdie, lost my footing, and landed in a rose bush—followed by a quick glare at the heavens. Little did my mother know, I thought, as I rubbed my knee that had had a close encounter with a hidden cement block and pulled thorns from my hands, that it seemed prayer could sometimes be painful.

The advice to pray had seemed so odd coming from my mother, whom I hadn't seen at prayer aside from the occasional nighttime prayer or lightning storm Rosary. The prayer card to St. Thérèse had actually come from a friend's mother, Mrs. Profetty. Whenever I spent the evening at her home, I'd notice that she'd excuse herself around nine o'clock and retreat to a softly lit corner in their parlor to pray. Once, when I asked her if she thought prayer worked, she answered with this verse from the Gospel of Matthew: "Ask, and it will be given you; seek, and you will find; knock, and it will be opened to you. For every one who asks receives, and he who seeks finds, and to him who knocks it will be opened" (Mt 7:7–8). This seemed like a good deal: rub the magic lantern, and out comes my genie with the three wishes. Got it! She then handed me a two by three prayer card with a young nun on the front and on the back a prayer I was to recite each morning before eleven o'clock for five days in a row. She referred to it as a novena—a prayer or series of prayers recited for nine days. As a girl with ADHD, I was excited to be offered this abridged version!

While the "magical" prayer card fascinated me, it was the scripture she quoted that piqued my curiosity. I found my Bible with wafer-thin pages from Confirmation, located Matthew's gospel, and read the passage she had shared with me. But it was the next verses that caught my attention and convinced me to give prayer a try. They read, "Or what man of you, if his son asks him for bread, will give him a stone? Or if he asks for a fish, will give him a serpent? If you then, who are evil, know how to give good gifts to your children, how much more will your Father who is in heaven give good things to those who ask him!" (7:9–11).

My angry glance at the heavens quickly turned into a bewildered look into myself. Sitting on the ground—nursing my swollen knee, scratched hands, and wounded pride—I wondered why the answer to this prayer hurt. I felt like I had presented a simple request to God, my Father. I wanted love plus the means to support and transport myself. In these desires, I saw peace, comfort, and freedom—all seemingly good things. Things I would assume a loving parent would want for his or her child, especially if it brought the child happiness. Instead, I got tossed into a rosebush. What was I missing? What could St. Thérèse possibly be trying to tell me by landing me mangled and entangled in a rose bush?

Hindsight is such a magnificent gift. Thirty years later, I am armed with a better appreciation of my faith, and although I may still wrestle with how God answers prayer, I never doubt that my eternal best interest is always foremost in those answers. I know that neither God nor St. Thérèse threw me into that rosebush—my horrendous badminton skills and overly competitive spirit did! As St. Paul teaches in his letter to the Romans, "Likewise the Spirit helps us in our weakness; for we do not know how to pray as we ought, but the Spirit himself intercedes for us with sighs too deep for words. And he who searches the hearts of men knows what is the mind of the Spirit, because the Spirit intercedes for the saints according to the will of God" (8:26–27).

The Spirit clearly "repackaged" my prayers for what was best for me. A few days after the rosebush incident, I remember thinking to myself that maybe I just needed to put aside my obsession with those items I believed would make me happy and focus on the things in my life that were presently bringing me joy. The answer to this first novena prayer was peace in my circumstances—an answer thankfully bestowed often on me throughout the years. But in God's perfect timing, I had all three of the things I wanted: the boyfriend (whose first gift to me was a single rose and who has since become "the husband"), the car (a surprise gift from my father), and multiple jobs!

St. Thérèse Novena for the Adoption Travel

September 21, 2009, we received news that they moved our travel date to adopt Faithy to October 29, 2009. I sent out so many requests begging the Lord in hopes that the date would somehow not be changed and we'd receive a miracle to be allowed to leave on September 24, 2009, instead. I finished the prayers for my novena to St. Thérèse, the one I'd been praying since I was a junior in high school, clutching the same sweet little prayer card. The answer, of course, was that my prayer was heard but not answered in my way—I had to trust this delay, like all the others, was part of God's perfect plan.

I love that my prayers are answered according to God's will and not according to mine, because in the end when we traveled was the absolute perfect time for us to go. I had prayed that we would be healthy during our travel, but if I had forced my way to go when I wanted to, that might not have been the case; swine flu ramped up during that time, and many people shared stories of being quarantined and not being able to leave China. I couldn't imagine being away from my boys any longer than the two weeks I was. We also would have traveled alone; instead, the Lord gave us as companions nine amazing families with whom we not only shared the journey but also forged a lifelong bond—to this day we weekend together with these families and refer to them as CAWLI cousins. It was also the support we needed during that time. I can't imagine Kevin and me alone in China trying to navigate this process.

One thing I learned from this experience is to be very careful interpreting signs and wonders. As I read my journal from that day with the hindsight of eleven years, I see how many times I was reading into emails and images and messages, wanting what I wanted, not being open to God's will. I'm so grateful that I did not force my way, assuming I had understood God, and instead continued to pray, seek his wisdom, and ask for his continued guidance. Turning to my guardian angel who enlightens, guides, and guards me, I know we were protected from our own agenda and desires to do things on our time and not trust in God.

God allowed me an interesting insight into a situation that may have contributed to the delay. During the wait, I went to adoration often; one day, I sat pouring my heart out to God, agonizing over the nearly six-month delay between when we received Faithy's photo and when we were allowed to travel to bring her home. In my heart, I felt a gentle whisper: "This adoption is not only about you. Her foster family needs more time. Be patient, and trust in me." Funny, until that moment, I'd not given the foster family a single thought. How easy it is to dehumanize a situation when you focus single-mindedly on what you want out of it!

The adoption paperwork we received from Faithy's home study from her foster care in China indicated that she was very attached to her foster father. It listed many examples of what appeared to be a very close bond between them, including him allowing her to use his phone. I don't know whether this man had any belief in God, but as we've seen in the scriptures, "the Spirit himself intercedes for us" (Rom 8:26). Perhaps there was a part of him struggling to let her go, and so

God in his lovingkindness allowed her to stay just a little bit longer while this man prepared his heart to say goodbye.

Stalked by St. Thérèse

Even though my first foray into praying a novena to St. Thérèse ended in the ER, I suppose a part of me never give up on prayer, it was just sporadic. How often did I misinterpret life's circumstances as a failure of prayer or a fault of God—as I first did when pulling the thorns from my hands the summer of my sophomore year in high school. Because I landed in a rose bush instead of landing a boyfriend, I inferred that God either doesn't really exist or he is punishing or mean-spirited. (PS: Neither is true: he is now and will forever be Love.) However, the prayer card bearing this express prayer for intercession from the saint known as the "Little Flower" remained dormant in the bottom of a keepsake box for many years. I've heard many Catholics claim to be "saint stalked"—that's when you find yourself with a special devotion to a saint who appeared in your life seemingly from nowhere. St. Thérèse falls into that category for me.

As I more fully embraced my Catholic faith in 2006, discovering the many amazing devotions and traditions, I became determined to build a "saint posse" filled with lesser-known holy men and women. I figured if I went for the more obscure saints, I'd have them all to myself for intercessions; I honestly didn't want to share their time with other people. Because everyone seemed to have a love for St. Thérèse, seeking those roses from heaven she promised to shower down, I didn't seek her out.

Yet as we prepared for Faithy's adoption, it became clear that St. Thérèse wanted to share this journey with us. Every piece of spiritual reading I chose included her. I'd be visiting a shrine or a church, suddenly feel her near, and turn to find her pictured either in the stained glass, on the wall, or as a statue. The real clincher came when I unearthed the precious prayer card, untouched and presumed lost for more than twenty years! *Okay, St. Thérèse, I'll give you a try.* The roses came flooding in, and she's been a member of the posse ever since.

One of the interesting details about Thérèse, especially since she spent most of her life in a cloister and died so young, is her title of Patron of Missionaries. She went on a pilgrimage to Rome with her family, a very engaging story of begging the pope to change her father's mind about allowing her to enter the convent. One of my favorite stories from that pilgrimage comes from her visit to the Colosseum: I'll let her tell you the story herself in this excerpt from *The Story of a Soul*:

> How shall I describe the feelings which thrilled me when I gazed on the Coliseum? At last I saw the arena where so many Martyrs had shed their blood for Christ. My first impulse was to kiss the ground sanctified by their glorious combats. But what a disappointment! The soil has been raised, and the real arena is now buried at the depth of about twenty-six feet.
>
> As the result of excavations the centre is nothing but a mass of rubbish, and an insurmountable barrier guards the entrance; in any case no one dare penetrate into the midst of these dangerous ruins. But was it possible to be in Rome and not go down to the real Coliseum? No, indeed! And I no longer listened to the guide's explanations: one thought only filled my mind—I must reach the arena. . . .
>
> As the warriors of old felt their courage grow in face of peril, so our joy increased in proportion to the fatigue and danger we had to face to attain the object of our desires. Céline, more foreseeing than I, had listened to the guide. She remembered that he had pointed out a particular stone marked with a cross, and had told us it was the place where the Martyrs had fought the good fight. She set to work to find it, and having done so we threw ourselves on our knees on this sacred ground. Our souls united in one and the same prayer. My heart beat violently when I pressed my lips to the dust reddened with the blood of the early Christians. I begged for the grace to be a martyr for Jesus, and I felt in the depths of my heart that my prayer was heard. All this took but a short time. After collecting some stones we approached the walls once more to face the danger. We were so happy that Papa had not the heart to scold us, and I could see that he was proud of our courage.[1]

After Thérèse's amazing intercession in securing a healthy and safe trip to China to bring Faithy home, I permanently added her to all of my travel plans! This included my pilgrimage to Rio de Janeiro in 2013 for World Youth Day with the Boston Deaf Apostolate and a more recent trip to speak in Fresno, California. I love the variety of ways Thérèse delivered her promised roses; when we were awaiting Faithy's arrival, each novena prayer was met with either an actual rose, a picture of a rose, or someone mentioning the word *rose*. In the later two trips, she became even more clever in making sure I remembered God never forsakes or abandons you, and she was praying alongside me every step of my anxiety-filled journeys!

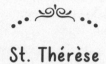

St. Thérèse

St. Thérèse, known as the Little Flower because of her "little way" of faith, promised to send a shower of roses upon the world, meaning she vowed to spend her time in heaven helping those on earth. Thérèse went home to the Lord at twenty-four after suffering for some time with tuberculosis; however, a mysterious illness in her childhood might have cut her life even shorter had it not been for a miracle brought about by the fervent prayers of her mother and a novena of Masses offered on her behalf.

During the Easter vacation in 1883, when Thérèse was ten years old, she was attacked by a mysterious illness with symptoms including trembling and frequent hallucinations. Worried for her young daughter, her mother, Zélie, requested a novena of Masses to be offered for Thérèse's cure. Miraculously, on Pentecost Sunday, May 13, 1883, Thérèse was suddenly cured.

Thérèse would reveal one more aspect of her miraculous healing. As her sisters knelt at her bedside praying, she looked at a statue of the Virgin Mary: "All of a sudden the Blessed Virgin appeared beautiful to me, so beautiful that never had I seen anything so attractive; her face was suffused with an ineffable benevolence and tenderness, but what penetrated to the very depths of my soul was the 'ravishing smile of the Blessed Virgin.' At that instant, all my pain disappeared, and two large tears glistened on my eyelashes, and flowed down my cheeks silently, but they were tears of unmixed joy."[2]

Mary's face was not the only one adored by Thérèse; she also held a special devotion to the image of Jesus's face left upon

Veronica's veil when she wiped his face with it along the Way of the Cross. She was so devoted, in fact, that the image was included in the name she took upon her vows to the Carmelites—Sr. Thérèse of the Child Jesus and the Holy Face. There even exists a photograph of Thérèse holding images of the Child Jesus and the Holy Face of Jesus. She described her attraction to this devotion in *Story of a Soul*: "He whose Kingdom is not of this world showed me that true wisdom consists in 'desiring to be unknown and counted as nothing,' in 'placing one's joy in the contempt of self.' Ah! I desired that, like the Face of Jesus, 'my face be truly hidden, that no one on earth would know me' (Is 53:3). I thirsted after suffering and I longed to be forgotten."[3]

Novenas

> For me, prayer is a burst from my heart, it is a simple
> glance thrown toward heaven, a cry of thanksgiving
> and love in times of trial as well as in times of joy.
> —*St. Thérèse of Lisieux*

The tradition of the novena goes back to when Mary prayed along with the apostles in the upper room for the nine days between the Ascension of Jesus and the descent of the Holy Spirit at Pentecost. Not only is a novena a great lesson in persistence in prayer, but it is also the joining of our prayers with those of the Church, the very essence of sacramentals.

One of the greatest obstacles to praying a novena is remembering to pray for five, nine, or even fifty-four days in a row. Over the years, I've developed a few sure-fire ways to keep me on the prayer track. The most obvious is to write it on your calendar—are you really going to skip a date with Jesus, the Blessed Mother, or one of your favorite saints? If I find the novena prayers online, I email them to myself every day, changing the subject line to the day of the novena until I finish. Now, I suppose this only works if you share my need to clean out my email every day. (Lingering emails make me edgy. My kitchen counter may have mountains of to-be-done items, but my email is spotless!) Another suggestion is to leave the prayer card or novena booklet out where you'll see it; probably one of the most logical places is next to the coffee maker. It seems that the adage "Out of sight, out of mind" can apply to prayer and practices of faith.

Adopting a More Tangible Faith

Growing in Grace with Scripture

> "Now Thomas, one of the twelve, called the Twin, was not with them when Jesus came. So the other disciples told him, "We have seen the Lord." But he said to them, "Unless I see in his hands the print of the nails, and place my finger in the mark of the nails, and place my hand in his side, I will not believe."
>
> Eight days later, his disciples were again in the house, and Thomas was with them. The doors were shut, but Jesus came and stood among them, and said, "Peace be with you." Then he said to Thomas, "Put your finger here, and see my hands; and put out your hand, and place it in my side; do not be faithless, but believing." Thomas answered him, "My Lord and my God!" Jesus said to him, "Have you believed because you have seen me? Blessed are those who have not seen and yet believe." (Jn 20:24–28)

One of the most poignant moments in John's Gospel comes from the meeting between Jesus and Thomas the Apostle after the Resurrection. "Doubting Thomas" refuses to accept the truth of Jesus's triumphant return until he has physically touched the wounds in his hands and side. In their exchange, we witness Jesus invite Thomas to touch, feel, see, and believe.

Connecting moments in scripture can help the faithful cultivate a more profound understanding from the blessing of, in essence, remembering the rest of the story. St. Elizabeth's words to Mary at the Visitation demonstrate a faithful response to God's promises and the markings of true faith. She says of Mary, "Blessed is she who believed that there would be a fulfilment of what was spoken to her from the Lord" (Lk 1:45)—words Jesus will echo in his exchange with Thomas thirty plus years later.

Mary believed in God's promise of a Messiah before experiencing the miraculous Resurrection—she was truly blessed by not needing physical evidence in order to accept the truth. She trusted in the prophecies and in the promises of God, recognizing that he is our ultimate salvation. Mary did not allow any obstacles to hinder her faith, and therefore she was blessed and she rejoiced.

How easily we can falter in our belief, looking for signs and wonders as prerequisites for believing. Obstacles to seeing and accepting the truth of God's promises fulfilled can mount daily if we fail to view the world with a heart willing to see God at work and embrace Jesus's glorious victory over sin, death, and the trouble of this world.

Mary allowed grace to fill every ounce of her being, strengthening her to give a daily yes to following and believing. Before Jesus even explained to the disciples that the work of God is to believe in the One sent by God (see John 6:29), Mary believed. As she stood before Elizabeth with the Fulfillment incubating within her, her Magnificat burst forth: "My soul magnifies the Lord; / and my spirit rejoices in God my Savior" (Lk 1:46–47).

We receive the same promises through the Eucharist; we see these mysteries unfold with Jesus literally within us every time we receive the Eucharist. The grace that filled every ounce of Mary's being is available to us abundantly; we merely need to ask, accept, and cooperate with it. "Ask, and it will be given you; seek, and you will find; knock, and it will be opened to you" (Mt 7:7). What keeps us from asking? Although St. Thomas is recorded as doubting, Jesus did not withhold from him what he asked for to help him believe.

Mary reminds us that God's "mercy is on those who fear him from generation to generation" (Lk 1:50). Believing without seeing, however difficult, is not impossible. God would never ask the impossible. He is a loving God who works the impossible within us through our cooperation with grace. No one exemplifies the powerful results of allowing ourselves to be filled with the grace of God more than the Blessed Virgin Mary. May we turn to her intercession, so that we too may be counted among the blessed who have not seen and yet believe.

Uncovering Grace

1. Do you have a daily prayer routine? Is there a special place you like to retreat to pray, read scripture, or have a quiet moment with the Lord? What types of prayer materials do you typically use in that time?
2. Did God ever answer a prayer in the most unexpected way, but the answer turned out to be far more advantageous than perhaps you were originally expecting when you prayed?
3. Do you have a saint posse? Although the list can be ever-changing, depending on our circumstances or new saintly discoveries, who are some of your current heavenly companions? Take a moment to contemplate why you have placed each of them in your inner prayer circle.

Grace–Building Activities

- Purchase laminated saint and prayer cards, and punch a hole in the top corner of each to create a prayer card ring. This is perfect for keeping toddlers and preschoolers occupied in Mass or even waiting in line at the supermarket. For adults, do the same with saints in your posse; hang the ring in your prayer corner, on your bed frame, or even in your car so you can easily turn to them throughout the day.
- Create a family prayer card. Create or choose a family novena to pray leading up to birthdays, wedding or death anniversaries, special occasions, or even a vacation (for safe travels or health during that time). You can use the computer or paper, markers, and whatever art supplies you have on hand to fashion your card.
- Collect saint cards as you would baseball cards. You can purchase special holders for your favorites. Create a family heirloom or keepsake journal where you can collect the cards, record stories as to why you chose those particular saints, and record any sweet encounters with or intercessions from your posse. Keep track of special events in your family or personal life, noting how the practice of your faith played a role in the day, the celebration, or even a vacation.

5

Covered in Love

St. Margaret Mary Alacoque, the Sacred Heart of Jesus, and the Brown Scapular

We must never be discouraged or give way to anxiety
. . . but ever have recourse to the adorable Heart of
Jesus.

—*St. Margaret Mary Alacoque*

Don't Leave Home without Them

If I can't leave home without my phone, keys, license, credit card (or
two), glasses, lipstick, and, let's face it, a purse full of other "essentials"
to feel complete, I should not try to navigate the big bad world without
a sacramental or two on hand to keep me connected to and reminded
of the most significant essential in my life—God! Sacramentals are
things we can carry and keep close that make us feel closer to our
true home.

These days my purse contents include a rosary (or two), a St.
Christopher medal (patron of travel), on occasion holy water, and a
"tiny saint" Ven. Patrick Peyton dangling from the zipper pull. I have
replaced my mini-Bible (yes, I carried one of those before they were
accessible via my phone—and before my eyes aged to the point of
inability to read anything below font size fourteen without magnifying
glasses!), with Biblegateway.com. Around my neck, I always wear a

crucifix, a Miraculous Medal, and a scapular. I love being a walking, albeit quiet, billboard for my beloved Catholic faith. If there were ever a Catholic *Let's Make a Deal*, I'd certainly be well prepared to play!

Yet it is even more important for me to leave home prepared to be open to the graces God may present to me that day, which equip me to tackle whatever situation my purse full of goodies cannot. Yes, that old American Express ad campaign was correct in reminding us, "Don't leave home without it," they just had "it" all wrong! Just as I once made the mistake of leaving Jesus in the church once Mass was over, for many years I also bid him farewell at the door of my home every time I ventured out. If I don't want Jesus to forget me for a minute or leave me behind, I must remember to return the favor. "But whoever denies me before men, I also will deny before my Father who is in heaven" (Mt 10:33)—that outcome would be, as they say, seriously *no bueno*. So, I tuck all those precious reminders, the sweet sacramentals of my Catholic faith, in the car, on my person, in my purse, on my phone, and all over my desk!

Extraordinary Graces

Flying nearly eight thousand miles one way despite my strong fear required an extraordinary outpouring of the grace of God and clinging to every promise my beloved sacramentals offered me. I was counting on the protection of the Blessed Virgin Mary, mainly on being covered in her veil of intercessory prayer and love. Clothed with a scapular and its promises, I felt a supernatural comfort and peace I'd never be able to attain on my own. Trust me; I'd tried many times before reverting to the faith!

Deacon Jerry Ryan blessed us on the Sunday before our departure for China on October 29th, in front of the entire church. I'll never forget that warm hug feeling I had, covered in that blessing as well as the prayers of the Church and the faithful at Mass that morning. I was reminded of the faithfulness of God—that even if all went awry, all would somehow still be well. Prayer is not about getting my way but about finding peace and joy in whatever God wills for my life. Not going to lie, though: I was more than happy and relieved that he and I were on the same page for this trip and the adoption!

Sacred Heart Devotion and Promises

How good and pleasant it is to dwell in the Heart
of Jesus! Who is there who does not love a heart so
wounded? Who can refuse a return of love to a Heart
so loving? Amen.

—St. Bernard of Clairvaux

The Promises of the Sacred Heart of Jesus to St. Margaret Mary:[1]

1. I will give them all the graces necessary in their state of life.
2. I will establish peace in their homes.
3. I will comfort them in all their afflictions.
4. I will be their secure refuge during life, and above all, in death.
5. I will bestow abundant blessings upon all their undertakings.
6. Sinners will find in my Heart the source and infinite ocean of mercy.
7. Lukewarm souls shall become fervent.
8. Fervent souls shall quickly mount to high perfection.
9. I will bless every place in which an image of my Heart is exposed and honored.
10. I will give to priests the gift of touching the most hardened hearts.
11. Those who shall promote this devotion shall have their names written in my Heart.
12. I promise you in the excessive mercy of my Heart that my all-powerful love will grant to all those who receive Holy Communion on the First Fridays in nine consecutive months the grace of final perseverance; they shall not die in my disgrace, nor without receiving their sacraments. My divine Heart shall be their safe refuge in this last moment.

Resting In Christ's Promises

Jesus shared with St. Margaret Mary in the 1670s, twelve promises
associated with devotion to his Sacred Heart. The one which drew me
into learning more about how to live this devotion in my life and home
was number nine, "I will bless every place in which an image of my
Heart is exposed and honored." As the reality of the adoption, travel to
China, and added responsibility of a child with special needs, emerged

with each paper signed, check mailed, and requirement fulfilled, my anxiety began to mount. The tension in our home intensified, as we each wrestled with fears and uncertainties of the impending changes as November 2009 drew closer. Kevin worried about the finances, I fretted over the travel, Ian wondered if his new sister would like him, and Adam struggled to relinquish his "baby of the family" title. In a desire to infuse grace into our home, and restore peace to our hearts, I sought more information on the Sacred Heart devotion. At that time, I purchased an icon of the Sacred Heart of Jesus and affixed it to the wall of our breakfast nook. This image is the sacramental tied to the devotion. (We'll cover more about holy art and images in chapter 8.) It was a start, and I loved the prominence of its placement (where it remains to this day), visible not only to our children during breakfast but to every visitor to our home.

The Devotion Practice after Bringing Faith Home

So how do I teach these devotions to Faithy to help her find the comfort I draw from them? I need to make them tangible. In my experience, much of what I pass on to my children stems from their witnessing my behavior—for better or worse. This applies especially to how they see me practice my Catholic faith—attending First Friday Masses, resting in the promises, being a positive example of living in the love of God. I'm not perfect at it, not even close, but I notice the closer I grow to Christ, especially through faithfully participating in my Catholic devotions, traditions, and practices, the more right the rest of my relationships are.

The extent, so far, of incorporating this beautiful devotion has been the placement of the Sacred Heart of Jesus image on the kitchen wall; and twice completing the nine First Friday Masses. Of these Masses, Jesus told St. Margaret, "I promise you in the unfathomable mercy of my heart that my omnipotent love will procure the grace of final penitence for all those who receive communion on nine successive first Fridays of the month; they will not die in my disfavor [the grace of final repentance], or without having received the sacraments, since my divine heart will be their sure refuge in the last moments of their life."[2]

Furthermore, I ordered the kit from the Sacred Heart Enthronement Network (WelcomeHisHeart.org) and keep looking for the perfect time to do the enthronement; however, that perfect time never
seems to come. An Enthronement, as described on the Welcome His
Heart website, is an action, involving prayer, by which one inaugu-
rates the beginning of Jesus having a throne in the life of someone or
a family. In writing this chapter, I have recognized the evil one's lies in
my assumption that the only good I can do in my faith is when I do it
perfectly. God does not ask for perfection, only faithfulness. The time
is now; especially with a deacon as a husband, I have no excuse. The
funny thing about us grace seekers is that we seem to feel we can only
partake partially from the abundance—as if we're saving our "God
wishes" in a magic lamp. God is no genie, as the promises from this
devotion show; we cannot out-pray his generosity.

The Comfort of the Brown Scapular

I have wrestled with anxiety for my entire life—more specifically, a
condition called mysophobia—most people know it as germophobia.
Mysophobia is often caused by a combination of biological, psycho-
logical, and environmental factors and is much more than a fear of
becoming ill; more precisely, it is the fear of contamination. Additionally, at a very young age, I developed a paralyzing fear of death,
perhaps driven by my father's numerous brushes with dying from his
heart condition beginning when I was nine. It certainly didn't help
when a drunk driver hit my car on the way to school, and the police
officer told my mother he was shocked I only had a broken nose. He
expected me to be dead, given the condition of the car. These little
things we hear and internalize, the negative thoughts and voices that
outweigh the hope from God, pushed me when my sons were small,
in the mid- to late 1990s, to a nearly agoraphobic state.

During a homeschool event I attended with my boys in 2004, I discovered the promises of the scapular, which comforted me and offered
me a hope like nothing had before. I knew it wasn't magic, that I had
to cooperate with grace; it prepared my heart to receive, reminding me
every time I reached down and felt first the cloth scapular and later,
in 2016, when eczema forced me to switch, the metal one. Death is
inevitable and for eternity; you cannot imagine the enormous weight

of fear Mary's words to Simon Stock lifted from my anxious heart. In a world I can control so little of, this promise of salvation, above all those I had yet discovered through sacramentals, secured my decision to follow Christ closer and to leave my wavering ways behind me.

The Perfect Name

So, what do sacramental devotions, a mother with anxiety, and naming your child have in common? Well, for me, they all came together when we chose *Faith* for our daughter's name. What an honor to bestow a name; Kevin and I put great thought into the names of our children; however, the boys were both born before my becoming more devout, so their names are more tied to culture than to the Church. My oldest is named for our fathers, and my younger son is named for two fabulous New England athletes and a special uncle. As the adoption journey unfolded, we realized the girls' names we had previously desired did not suit the little girl for whom we were waiting.

As a woman with acute, sometimes paralyzing anxiety, to travel out of the country for the first time, halfway around the world, to bring home a three-year-old child with special needs, would take an enormous amount of faith. Although the seed for the desire to adopt had been planted many years ago, the reality in the moment was petrifying. How would I complete the good work God had begun through me? There wasn't anything or anyone on earth who could give me the strength, courage, and grace to fulfill the beautiful work of giving this child a home and a family; it was God alone.

As we continued to pray ourselves through this process, in early 2007, it become clear that the only name for our little girl was *Faith*. After we read Hebrews 11:1—"Now faith is the assurance of things hoped for, the conviction of things not seen"—any lingering doubt faded away. This verse also affirmed for us the dynamic, living reality of the Word of God; I love how the Spirit uses scripture to speak words we can see into the prayer we cannot. Hebrews 11 speaks of the faith we hold in God as the assurance of what we cannot see and the certainty of what we hope in. That was precisely how I felt about my daughter and the promise of her joining our family one day. I could not see her, but I knew she was there; even before we had an actual match. No matter how long the delay, I encountered peace in my faith and in this once unfathomable dream to be this little girl's mother.

Interestingly, the Deaf culture possesses an incredible name-bestowing tradition. Instead of finger spelling a person's name every time you are introducing, referring to, or even speaking with them, some Deaf use sign names. This name, which can only be assigned by someone who is deaf or hard of hearing, often reflects a special or unique attribute of the person. Since we had yet to make Deaf friends, and out of respect for the naming custom, we provisionally assigned the ASL sign for *faith* to our daughter. For all the reasons I mentioned, it definitely seemed fitting!

As Faithy grew to understand more of the Catholic faith and saw me use that particular sign in my interpreting of the Mass, it helped, in some small way, illustrate the meaning of her name and why we choose it for her. She received her official ASL sign name a year after she began attending an all-Deaf private school. A touching collaboration between her amazing new Deaf community, teachers, friends, and embracing her Deaf culture, her sign makes reference to her dimple when she smiles and her innate friendliness. Another perfectly fitting name!

St. Margaret Mary Alacoque

St. Margaret Mary Alacoque, born on July 22, 1647, in L'Hautecour, Burgundy, France experienced visions of Jesus Christ for most of her life.[3] Her early life was marked with great difficulties, including losing her father when she was nine just after he had been betrayed by a business partner, which meant the family would live in great poverty. Margaret suffered from a rheumatic fever, which left her temporarily paralyzed. Although during her illness she vowed virginity, once well she soon forgot the promise and began attending balls and socializing, and even contemplated marriage. One night, she had a vision of the scourged Jesus; this reignited her vow to Jesus, and in May 1671 she entered religious life at the Visitation Convent at Paray-le-Monial.

It was during her time in this monastery that Margaret received several private revelations of the Sacred Heart of Jesus. These visions showed her the form and chief features of the Sacred Heart devotion as well as the celebration of the Feast of the Sacred Heart to be held the Friday after the octave of Corpus Christi, usually in June.

Margaret spent many years trying to convince her order of the validity of her apparitions, eventually doing so through the help of her Jesuit confessor, Claude de la Colombière. After serving as novice mistress and assistant superior, Margaret Mary died on October 17, 1690, at the age of forty-three, while receiving the sacrament of the Anointing of the Sick. Margaret's poignant final words were "I need nothing but God, and to lose myself in the heart of Jesus."

The Brown Scapular

"Whoever dies invested with this scapular shall be preserved from the eternal flames. It is a sign of salvation, a sure safeguard in danger, a pledge of peace and of my special protection until the end of the ages."
~ *Our Lady of Mount Carmel appeared to Carmelite monk St. Simon Stock in 1251 and presented him with a brown wool scapular*

This sacramental is a tangible symbol of the incredible reality of the protection of the Blessed Mother offers under her own mantle. According to the Vatican, "The Scapular of Mount Carmel is a reduced form of the religious habit of the Order of the Friars of the Blessed Virgin of Mount Carmel. Its use is very diffuse and often independent of the life and spirituality of the Carmelite family."[4]

The scapular is an external sign of the filial relationship established between the Blessed Virgin Mary, Mother and Queen of Mount Carmel, and the faithful who entrust themselves totally to her protection, who have recourse to her maternal intercession and are mindful of the primacy of the spiritual life and the need for prayer.[5]

Do not fear wearing the scapular "imperfectly"; the disposition of your heart is what truly matters. We clothe ourselves in the devotion to be reminded of Mary's love for us but also because of our desire to draw close to Mary, which in turn brings us ever closer to her Son, Jesus. There are many other types of scapulars, but it is the brown one that is most familiar and that was given by the Blessed Mother, under the title of Our Lady of Mount Carmel, to Simon Stock.

On December 16, 1910, Pope St. Pius X made an official decree allowing a scapular medal to be substituted, in most cases, for any of the various scapulars. However, valid enrollment, which may only be done by a priest or a deacon, must be completed before making the substitution.

Adopting a More Tangible Faith

Growing in Grace with Scripture

> And from there he [Jesus] arose and went away to the region of Tyre and Sidon. And he entered a house, and would not have any one know it; yet he could not be hid. But immediately a woman, whose little daughter was possessed by an unclean spirit, heard of him, and came and fell down at his feet. Now the woman was a Greek, a Syrophoeni'cian by birth. And she begged him to cast the demon out of her daughter. And he said to her, "Let the children first be fed, for it is not right to take the children's bread and throw it to the dogs." But she answered him, "Yes, Lord; yet even the dogs under the table eat the children's crumbs." And he said to her, "For this saying you may go your way; the demon has left your daughter." And she went home, and found the child lying in bed, and the demon gone. (Mk 7:24–30)

I am a grace beggar, much like the Syrophoenician woman in Mark's Gospel. I'll take the scraps because I know they are more than enough to heal us. The very least that Jesus has to give us could completely transform our lives. Imagine if we embraced even a tiny bit of the blessings and graces that Jesus offers us—how would our lives be? How much unnecessary anxiety, confusion, and apprehension have I allowed into my life because I doubted the power of even the smallest spiritual scrap? The gifts available from heaven are abundant, so we do not need to settle for the crumbs, yet if that were all we allowed ourselves to dine upon we'd still be filled. Although our lives would not be perfect or free from those things that worry, concern, or pain us, we would feel a release of those that possess our thoughts and time and discover a sense of inner peace and hope that can only come from heaven. The woman came to Jesus prepared to be persistent, humble, and assured. Her persistence was clearly evident by her willingness to beg for satisfaction. She showed her humility in addressing Jesus as Lord and taking whatever scraps were offered. She demonstrated her confidence that what he said was done had truly been done by leaving for home at his command. When was the last time I approached Jesus in that way—begging for some assistance, humbled by his majesty and glory, and yet completely sure that I would in some way receive a blessing—either the one I thought I needed or the one he knew I needed?

Uncovering Grace

1. Have you ever considered yourself a grace beggar? In what circumstances do you most find yourself praying for an outpouring of grace from God?
2. Which sacramental devotions do you regularly participate in? What drew you to these particular devotions? How have they helped strengthen your faith?
3. Which of the twelve Sacred Heart promises speaks comfort into a current trying situation in your life? In what ways can you rest your head on Jesus's heart—obviously not in the physical way St. Margaret was permitted to in December 1673, but in a spiritual sense that will in turn make the grace of this devotion more tangible?

Grace-Building Activities

- Participate in an Enthronement to the Sacred Heart in your home, parish, school, or workplace. WelcomeHisHeart.com has enthronement kits and digital downloads (there is a suggested donation for each). Enthronement, according to the website, is "a fulfillment of a request Jesus made to St. Margaret Mary in the 1670s when He said, 'I will bless every place in which an image of my Heart is exposed and honored.'"[6] The entire family does not have to be present or even completely on board for you to enthrone your home, nor does it require clergy. Learn more on the Welcome His Heart website.

- Create your own scapular. There are kits for those who sew as well as for those who do not. There are patterns to follow or even precut versions to assemble. Once again, I have to go with Catholic Icing, www.catholicicing.com/catholic-scapular-crafts-diys for the win!

- Learn the history of the brown scapular. Visit a church dedicated to Our Lady of Mount Carmel or a Carmelite shrine. July 16 is the Feast Day for Our Lady of Mount Carmel; for that day, you could plan a special celebration, arrange for the investiture, or brainstorm with your family items to include in a celebratory meal. A few years ago, I helped organize a three-day mission at our diocese's Our Lady of Mount Carmel church. We invited a musician and a guest speaker, who both agreed to be paid their honoraria based on the donations collected (each received a fair day's wage). The mission ended with investiture in the brown scapular.

6

My Weapon of Choice

Ven. Patrick Peyton and the Rosary

With the Rosary, the Christian people sits at the school of Mary and is led to contemplate the beauty on the face of Christ and to experience the depths of his love. Through the Rosary the faithful receive abundant grace, as though from the very hands of the Mother of the Redeemer.

—*Pope St. John Paul II*

Nighttime Rosary Memories

My earliest memories of the Rosary originate from my childhood. My mother was petrified of thunder and lightning storms. My father worked the night shift, so she was home alone with us three children most of the time. During storms, we would run around the house unplugging all our electronics (remember when that was possible?). Then she would line us up on the couch and we would pray the Rosary—just the Our Fathers and Hail Marys, not even sure we included the Glory Be, and we definitely didn't talk about the Mysteries. Then our house was struck by lightning—true story. The house was fine, but a little bit of my belief that prayer could protect me was shattered, and I don't believe we ever prayed the Rosary as a family again.

My grandmother, however, would reinvigorate my desire to spend time praying the Rosary. I would often get homesick when I spent the night at her house. Since she lived too far from my parents for me to go home if I got scared in the middle of the night, she would bring me a little plastic rosary to hold and to pray until I fell asleep. At first, I thought, *You're right, Grammie, this is perfect; the boredom will have me asleep in no time!* It would be years before I realized the wisdom of my grandmother and the Rosary. Prayer is comforting, and I often think of holding the rosary as holding Mary's hand; to this day, even if I am too overwhelmed, sad, or anxious to say the words of the prayers, I can hold tight to my rosary and know that Mary is near.

My grandmother understood the peace from our time praying with Mary, a legacy I am so grateful she passed on to me. As I move the beads through my fingers, reciting those familiar prayers, the most amazing thing happens. Somehow, I am able to recite the words while simultaneously contemplating the Mysteries of the Rosary. Every time I pick up one of my fifty-plus strings of beads, I feel in my heart the Blessed Mother guiding me through her Son Jesus's birth, life, death, and Resurrection.

In his 2002 apostolic letter *Rosarium Virginis Mariae*, Pope St. John Paul II referred to the Rosary as where the faithful sit in the "school of Mary" (14). The pope captures how the Rosary is indeed Mary's prayer when he states, "Mary lived with her eyes fixed on Christ, treasuring his every word: 'She kept all these things, pondering them in her heart' (Lk 2:19; cf. 2:51). The memories of Jesus, impressed upon her heart, were always with her, leading her to reflect on the various moments of her life at her son's side. In a way those memories were to be the 'rosary' which she recited uninterruptedly throughout her earthly life" (11).

The Rosary is no longer my bedtime sedative. Wanting to be fully present, I usually walk as I pray the Rosary. These twenty minutes or so become my one-on-one tutoring sessions with the Blessed Mother, the most outstanding homeschool teacher of all time. This mystical instruction with the one who knew Jesus best instills wisdom, peace, and joy within my soul.

Overcoming Rejection

In preparation for Faithy's adoption, we learned that a normal reaction in adopted children is to select one parent to begin bonding with, while in essence rejecting the other. That rejected one turned out to be me. Kevin saw the blessing in that, given our personalities; if it had been reversed, he doesn't believe he would have worked as hard as I did to build trust and a relationship with her, at least not while in China. He would have gone sightseeing, assuming she'd eventually come around. I, however, am stubborn, and after this long wait and my overwhelming desire for her to accept me as her mom, I knew I had work to do.

First, to build that trust bond, it was crucial for Faithy to see me as the source of her every physical need. Food, drink, clothes, baths, toileting, toys—everything had to come from me. I knew this would build our bond over time. Trust builds when a need arises and is then quickly and appropriately tended to—over and over and over again. Every time I looked into her eyes, my heart ached for her to know the truth of what was happening—so I prayed the Rosary, in essence holding Mary's hand and letting her mother me as I worked so hard to mother my new daughter.

One night, we lay down at eight thirty and prayed the Rosary as a family. I attempted to sign a few Our Fathers and Hail Marys when she'd look at me, though I knew these hand gestures meant nothing to her at this point. However, it was apparent God was doing something mystical behind the scenes as I watched her gaze fall on the crucifix dangling from her new daddy's rosary. I stopped signing and let her heavenly Father teach her the prayers with words I'll never know this side of heaven.

We prayed for our health, our safety, strength, and wisdom; we prayed for healing on this poor child whose prior life was a mystery to us but included trauma and loss. We prayed for the opportunity to be workers in his vineyard and for the incredible love God must have for us to use our dreams of having a daughter (and) to do his will. Our heavenly Father so loves us that, although struggles will abound in varying amounts, his love will manifest beyond measure!

Every time anxiety crept back into my heart, I fell to my knees, feeling even closer to heaven beside the window of our twenty-fourth–floor hotel room. I prayed for strength, peace in my circumstances, and his will to be done in all things. I invoked the Holy Spirit, the Blessed Mother, and my entire saint posse, begging for their intercession. Prayer carries power far more immense than any fear of the unknown or of plans not going exactly how you expected. Never in my life have I needed more that comfort of holding the beads of the rosary, imagining I was holding Mary's hand, than in the days we spent in China.

Strength from Praying the Rosary

Bonds between mother and child are established through contact, particularly skin-to-skin. With Faithy, who early in our China trip continued to want nothing to do with me, we decided to work on bonding by taking baths with her, especially after discovering her fondness for the tub. I slipped on my bathing suit, and she joined me, though somewhat begrudgingly, and cried through most of it. There were moments of calm, and every now and then she'd scoot back against me as a sign that she at least viewed me as a safety net in this deep water even if she was still unsure of letting me in.

I gave her a little back rub as I washed her back, noting how much she loved the massage. My heart wondered if she'd ever been lavished with so much attention and care. I rubbed her skinny legs, shocked by the lack of muscle and the outward curve of her adorable, unusually proportioned little feet. We cried together, and I prayed a lot (repeating the Hail Mary continually in my head), hoping for any breakthrough in her seeing me as her mother. I continued to focus on fulfilling all her personal care needs and not pushing an emotional bond. I wanted to give her a chance to process and open up on her own.

The next day, as Faithy sat cuddling with daddy in the chair, I decided to shower. To our amazement, as I left the room, she came waddling after me. She went right to the tub, looked at me, and pointed inside. Delighted, I changed my plans to the blessing of another bath bonding session with my daughter. As I began to run the water, she trustingly put her hands up for me to remove her jammies. My heart leaped; could she really be seeking a bonding experience with me—on her own? *Please, Lord*, I prayed, *guide my every move*. We got in, and she backed right up against me; I heard a whimper or two, but she wanted to be there. I repeated the last night's routine of back rub and back wash; adorably, she nearly fell asleep! She appeared completely calm and relaxed for the first time since we brought her back to the hotel, giving us time together without crying. Kevin was in the room this time, but she didn't reach for him or try to escape; she just lay against me as I rubbed those skinny legs and long toes. And yes, we cried again, but this time it was only the two big ones—the little one was just soaking up the tub and the love!

Baby steps, but Kevin and I cherished the glimmer of what we hoped would blossom into the long-awaited turning point. There would be many more tears, trials, and tantrums (from both of us). Still, we'd take the small wins—her allowing shows of affection from me such as kisses on her forehead, a significant reduction of the turned-up faces of disgust she was giving me when I approached, and even allowing physical touch from me outside of the bathtub.

My journal reveals how my heart overflowed at how you can love so much someone whom you know so little about, having met only three days earlier. It reminded me, in a way, of the relationship between God and us. When we are adopted into the family of God and loved by him unconditionally, how he must long for us to bond with and trust in him as we fight against his gestures of love. I am grateful for his infinite patience, knowing he'd never give up on me, much as I'd never give up on building my parental relationship with Faithy.

Something for Everyone

"Prayer is the raising of one's mind and heart to God or the requesting of good things from God" (*CCC* 2559). While prayer may not change our circumstances, it continually changes our hearts. It brings us closer to God in a way that allows him to comfort us, guide us, and occasionally reveal his plan for us. At the very least, communication with God always brings peace. The Catholic faith offers many beautiful devotions able to reach the faithful, who come to prayer with many different communication styles. God created each of us to be unique and unrepeatable; therefore, it stands to reason that he would provide a multitude of ways for us to communicate with him.

The Rosary checks off so many tangible prayer experiences for me. My rosary beads give me something to fidget with, the prayers offer me things to think about (and hear if I am praying aloud), and when I use my rose-scented beads, they provide me a beautiful smell. A devotion I have struggled my entire Catholic life, as a child and again after my reversion in 2005, to incorporate into my prayer life has become one of the greatest gifts. Honestly, it was not until I was hired by Family Rosary in 2022, whose whole mission is to promote family prayer, primarily through the Rosary, that it became a daily habit—I didn't want to be a hypocrite (well played Mama Mary, well played). The Rosary gives me something to (literally) hold on to, especially when I'm in the midst of a struggle. There have been times when the words of the prayers would not come, yet merely holding this beautiful sacramental brought me comfort and hope.

Meditating upon the Mysteries of the Rosary in the school of Mary, we learn so much about who Jesus is and how he wants to be a part of our lives. Furthermore, in meditating with Mary upon the life of Jesus, we learn that she had many adversities yet never lost her joy and her hope. Praying with her to Our Lord provides us an opportunity to grow in faith guided by a loving mother.

Teaching Faithy the Rosary

The Rosary was one of the ways we began communicating our faith to Faithy. When we were teaching her the prayers in ASL, a friend even crocheted one red and ten blue roses so we could count the prayers while keeping our hands free to sign. It would take years before we could expand from the prayers to the Mysteries, but as with my journey with the Rosary, the prayers and the comfort of the beads were enough until she was ready to go deeper.

Mary is always waiting to teach us about her beloved Son and the unspeakable joy, sorrow, light, and glory of the Rosary Mysteries. Even when I wasn't sure what Faithy was absorbing from our time together praying, I knew that the grace of that time in prayer was teaching her things far beyond what this world could teach. St. Paul's words from Philippians 4:13, "I can do all things through Christ who strengthens me," were how I perceived that time in prayer. It would indeed be years before Faithy understood the words of the Our Father, the Glory Be, and the Hail Mary, and the Creed would take even longer. But she knew the comfort of that time in prayer; she knew who we were praying to, and that for me was enough. The repetition of the prayers was a way for me to enforce the learning of the prayers, and over time I would find beautiful children's books with illustrations that brought the Mysteries to life. One series even included rose graphics along the bottom of the page, which meant I could pray for her with my hands reading aloud while her finger kept track of where we were on the rosary.

Even though she still cannot pray this beautiful prayer alone, she can pray it with the Church. She too can hold the beads, as if she is holding Mary's hand as she is guided in prayer.

The lessons contained in the Mysteries of the Rosary on who Jesus is and how we should be are what I want to pass along to my daughter. Embracing every grace and blessing God offers is so important, yet with her cognitive limitations, I can only do so much. Still, I believe with my whole heart that all of heaven communicates with (and blesses) Faithy in ways I will never understand but for which I am eternally grateful.

Saints for the Journey

Once again, our journey with the sacramental came with a saint friend. In 2005, as my reversion unfolded daily, my friend Christin introduced me to Fr. Patrick Peyton, the Rosary Priest, and the Father Peyton Center, just minutes from my home. I attended Rosary, Mass, Confession, and made frequent visits to Fr. Peyton's grave, as I navigated this new chapter in my Catholic faith. He seems to have adopted me and my family, as well, for we'd see many answered prayers through his intercession, not only while waiting to bring her home from China, but I the years to follow.

It was a priceless gift to introduce my daughter to Fr. Patrick Peyton, bringing her to visit and pray by his grave then spending time at the Museum of Family Prayer at Stonehill College south of Boston, which teaches about the Rosary and Fr. Peyton's amazing life. Our family was even included in their video board presentations on prayer when it first opened. How overjoyed Faithy was to see this six-foot screen of herself sharing in her native ASL, how she uses prayer to grow closer to Christ.

In June 2018, my husband, Kevin, and I were included in the liturgy to celebrate Pope Francis's promulgation of the decree recognizing the heroic virtues of Fr. Peyton, thus finding him venerable in the Roman Catholic Church. Our role included participating in the Mass procession and dressing the altar—we laid the linens upon the altar before the Liturgy of the Eucharist began. Although Mass was the day's true highlight, coming in a very close second was sitting next to and speaking with Fr. Peyton's cousins at lunch. Fr. Peyton's latest intercession included an unexpected opportunity in 2022 to join the Family Rosary team as an employee guiding their digital and social media content—more fruit, I believe, of praying the Rosary.

Ven. Patrick Peyton, the Rosary Priest

Patrick Peyton was born in Ireland in 1909, in Attymass, County Mayo. Fr. Peyton recounted many times how his family prayed the Rosary together each night, which helped him develop a solid foundation of faith. He would lean on this throughout his formation to priesthood with the Congregation of Holy Cross.[1]

Fr. Patrick Peyton, CSC, came to the United States as a young man and devoted his priestly life to spreading devotion to Mary and encouraging family prayer, especially the Rosary. His promotion of the Rosary devotion, a promise he made to our Blessed Mother after her intercession brought his miraculous healing from tuberculosis in 1938, would lead to his moniker as "the Rosary Priest." He hosted more than 500 rallies in the United States and across the globe to encourage family prayer and devotion to the Rosary. Peyton died in 1992, and the Vatican opened his cause for canonization in 2001; in 2017, Pope Francis recognized the heroic virtue of Patrick Peyton's life and declared him "Venerable."

Today, Fr. Peyton's messages that "The family that prays together stays together" and "A world at prayer is a world at peace" are known around the world. Because he was a man of great virtue, his cause for sainthood was officially opened in 2001.

Fr. Peyton is one of many amazing, virtuous people who, although they never encountered the divine in apparition form, still believed with a conviction that allowed them to build a genuine relationship with Jesus, Mary, and Joseph, among other heavenly friends. His devotion stands as an example to all ordinary men and women that through the power of prayer, especially family prayer, we can all enjoy the friendship, protection, and love of the Holy Family in our lives.

History of the Rosary

> When I needed her and her power and her friendship, she didn't forget that ever since I had been a little child and could open my mouth, I had used that power to say the Rosary; so when I needed her friendship, she was glad to give it to me.
>
> —*Ven. Patrick Peyton, CSC*

St. Dominic, the founder of the Dominicans, has long been connected to the spread of the Rosary devotion, especially in the form we now pray it. There is substantial evidence that he added to existing devotions that involved the counting of prayers, first done by monks using rocks to keep track of their daily psalter prayers, by creating meditations on the life of Christ. Interestingly, there seems to be no documentation from the early thirteenth century to prove or disprove St. Dominic's connection with the Rosary; the meticulous depositions taken from eyewitnesses during the investigation of his life for his canonization process, although they mention many of his miracles and revelations, say nothing about the Rosary.[2]

Regardless of this clouded history of his involvement in the origin of the Rosary, there is no debating St. Dominic's personal devotion and preaching on the importance of praying the Rosary and seeking the Blessed Mother's intercession. This is known through St. Dominic's appearance to the fifteenth-century Dominican priest Bl. Alain de la Roche (Alan of the Rock) urging a renewed preaching of the Rosary devotion because it would bear fruit and save souls. It is these words spoken to Bl. Alain that help forever connect the Rosary with St. Dominic. St. Dominic told Bl. Alain of the great results of his own ministry: he had preached the holy Rosary unceasingly, his sermons had borne great fruit, and many people had been converted during his missions. He said to Bl. Alain, "See the wonderful results I have had through preaching the holy Rosary! You and all those who love Our Lady ought to do the same so that, by means of this holy practice of the Rosary, you may draw all people to the real science of the virtues."[3]

Adopting a More Tangible Faith

Growing in Grace with Scripture

> I have said this to you, that in me you may have peace. In the world you have tribulation; but be of good cheer, I have overcome the world. (Jn 16:33)

All five Joyful Mysteries of the Rosary can be found in the first and second chapters of Luke's gospel. The first decade corresponds to the Annunciation (Lk 1:26–38); the second to the Visitation (Lk 1:39–56); followed by the Birth of Our Lord (Lk 2:1–20); the Presentation at the Temple (Lk 2:22–38); and the Finding in the Temple (Lk 2:41–52). Reading these accounts in scripture enhances our praying of the Rosary. It also lays out for us the intermingling of Mary's joys with her sorrows and offers the grace to understand the difference between joy and happiness.

During our adoption journey, we had many experiences of the joy of waiting and anticipation—even in being with our new daughter—mingled with distress and difficulties. I clung to my rosary and the Blessed Mother through all of it because I knew she had experienced the roller coaster ride that is parenting in a far more extreme way, and never lost her hope, trust, and most of all, faith in God. How could I, after witnessing such an incredible example in her life, not turn to this role model as a resource for remaining hopeful and at peace in our journey? Happiness is fleeting and dependent on circumstances; joy is dependent on the Lord, who never abandons, forsakes, or fails to be with us. Joy is eternal and unshakable; happiness is in the present moment. And while God does delight in giving us the desires of our hearts in the here and now, he is far more concerned with and rejoices in offering us the eternal crown of glory!

Whatever circumstance you currently find yourself in, take heart in Jesus's words: "I have said this to you, that in me you may have peace. In the world you have tribulation; but be of good cheer, I have overcome the world" (Jn 16:33)!

Uncovering Grace

1. What is your earliest memory of praying the Rosary? Do you remember who introduced you to it? (Side note: It might be nice to tuck that person and his or her intentions into your next Rosary as a big thank-you. If this chapter is your introduction, I gladly accept prayer donations for my family.)
2. Contemplating the power of praying the Rosary to bring an end to the war, as Mary instructed the children at Fatima, what conflicts in your life do you need to cover in Mary's mantle and the prayers of the Rosary? How does this image of the praying of the Rosary to end wars in your heart, home, community, and world, bring peace or restore hope in those situations?
3. How do you pray the Rosary—in the car, before bed, during a walk? Do you find this devotion, or any of those mentioned in this book, difficult to make a holy habit? Brainstorm ways to incorporate prayer into your daily life. Consider a technique referred to as bundling—putting together something you have to do, like the dishes, with something you'd like to do, like offering a Hail Mary for each member of your family! Having multiple possibilities gives you flexibility and makes it easier to accomplish your goals each day.

Grace-Building Activities

• Buy a rosary-making kit. You can find them for both adults and kids. Can you crochet or knit? There are patterns to create ten roses in one color and one in another so your child can follow along at any age; these were particularly helpful for our family. There are also instructions online for making knotted rosaries, particularly effective companions for the Our Lady Undoer of Knots Novena.[4]

- Pray for different people and intentions with each bead. Recall a particular person and/or intention; if it helps, organize intentions from decade to decade—praying for ten women having babies; ten neighbors from my childhood; or ten people in need of work or new jobs. Not only does this methodology keep you focused to finish the Rosary, but more important, you've now covered more than fifty people in much-needed prayers!

- Take a Rosary walk. You can do this either around your neighborhood, in a park, or, if you are blessed enough, at a local shrine or church. In our area, several young men have created Rosary gardens and walks as Eagle Scout projects. I even have friends who created their own in the woods behind their house. Combining walking and praying not only is a great way of bundling two very important things to do every day but also, at least in my experience, cuts down on distractions from domestic duties, the phone, or the computer screen with the next task beckoning.

7

Inspired by the Word

St. John the Evangelist, the Blessed Mother, and Scripture

Few souls understand what God would accomplish in them if they were to abandon themselves unreservedly to him and if they were to allow His grace to mold them accordingly.
—*St. Ignatius Loyola*

A Budding Bible Obsession

Before 2004, the only Bible I owned was a red-covered copy with wafer-thin paper that was handed out during Confirmation preparation. Since a lady never reveals her age, let's say that was a very long time ago. But that all changed with a simple Christmas gift: a woman from my parish who barely knew me gave me a book on the scriptures and how those help build a relationship with Jesus. She didn't stop there; the unexpected gift came with an enthusiastic invitation to join a Bible study at her home. Truth be told, convinced that Catholics didn't read the Bible, I called it a book club for nearly three years.

The Holy Spirit is just amazing, if you haven't had the opportunity to notice yet. I'm grateful for the gentle nudges the Holy Spirit gives me toward sanctification, otherwise known as holiness. If this friend had merely invited me to the "book club," I probably wouldn't have accepted; however, with the gift of the book in my hands I definitely felt obligated to at least try the new group. I grew up being taught that religion is private, something you don't share; this idea of coming together with other women to discuss faith, the Bible, and our feelings felt foreign and quite frankly scary!

Through this sweet soul's desire to share what she found in Christ, a whole new world was about to unfold before me—not all at once, but this first step was all the Spirit needed. Although I thought I had let Jesus into my life when I returned to attending the Catholic Church in 1991, I was about to find that there was a rich treasury of traditions and devotions I had barely begun to tap. Truthfully, I didn't know the breadth of things about the Church I didn't know.

After going to the first meeting and discovering that women's groups come with yummy snacks such as cupcakes and guacamole, I returned every week, more for the food than for Jesus at first. Eventually, the ember in my heart, fueled by the scriptures and a budding relationship with Jesus, ignited into a firestorm. I could never have imagined, nor could I ever have contained, the passionate faith that was brewing. However, I'm getting ahead of myself; suffice it to say that what I classify as a slight obsession with Bibles—a collection that now occupies a couple of rows on my bookshelf—all began with this invitation and my discovery of the scriptures.

A Special Place in My Heart

St. John the Evangelist has a special place in my heart, one he held long before I knew I would one day also be an evangelist. Looking back, I'm not sure what exactly drew me to him at first, but I'm reasonably sure it has to do with his relationship and connection with Mary. I can't help but be in awe of John's willingness to immediately take Mary into his home after his friend Jesus asked from the Cross. She was already a fixture in his life from his travels with her Son; now he took her into his home; and later Mary and the apostles would all spend that special time together in the upper room. It seems only inevitable that Mary would have a special place in John's heart as well as his home.

As his dying wish expressed in front of the people witnessing his Crucifixion, Jesus entrusted John with the unique charge of caring for his mother: "When Jesus saw his mother, and the disciple whom he loved standing near, he said to his mother, 'Woman, behold, your son!' Then he said to the disciple, 'Behold, your mother!' And from that hour the disciple took her to his own home" (Jn 19:26–27). And in that moment, he gave each of us to Mary as her spiritual (dare I say adopted?) children. Perhaps it was this relationship that piqued my interest, especially as I began to discern my own call to adopt a child.

I was intrigued by John referring to himself as "the disciple whom [Jesus] loved" right before he recorded Jesus's request, "Behold, your mother!" (Jn 19:27). The *Didache Bible* explains it this way: "In entrusting the care of his Mother to the beloved disciple and entrusting the disciple to his Mother, Christ established Mary as the Mother of the Church and, therefore, the spiritual Mother of every Christian believer; the disciple 'whom Jesus loved' is often said to represent the entire body of the Church."[1] Even though I knew none of this as I first read those words for my Bible study homework, I felt it in my heart. John's encounter with the Blessed Mother became my encounter as well.

To Be Known and Loved

Through studying the Gospel of John in that initial faith sharing group, I saw the Bible as God's love letter to me for the first time. While the entire Bible is divinely inspired: "All scripture is inspired by God and is profitable for teaching, for reproof, for correction, and for training in righteousness, that the man of God may be complete, equipped for every good work" (2 Tm 3:16–17)—it was John's writings in particular that moved my heart closer to Jesus. His Gospel broke open the idea that God loved me—not just people in general, but me personally. Through John's letters, particularly 1 John 4:16, the fearful little girl inside me learned that I could not only "know and believe the love God has for us" but, as the *New International Version* puts it, *rely* on that love. While it was important to believe in God's love for me, Bible study unfolded an entirely new level of the faith, helping me realize I could fully *rely* on that love was life changing.

That love would also strengthen me to make decisions and agree to God's mission for my life. Within three years of being invited to that Bible study, I would enter some of my darkest days, as the very friendships that brought me to scripture and a relationship with Jesus began to disintegrate. Just as John must have been confounded at the foot of the Cross at what he thought God's plan for his future was, I was suffering from great confusion because I thought these friends that God had brought to my life were his answer to my prayer to grow closer to him. By then, my love and reliance on scripture had reached beyond St. John to St. Paul and others; at this time, it was the words of Romans 8:28, "We know that in all things God works for the good of those who love him, who have been called according to his purpose," that became a life preserver of hope as my Bible study friends left the Church, and me, behind. I had to wrestle with my own decision on where to worship; follow my friends to this new non-denominational faith or remain Catholic. The decision could not be based on where I'd have more friends; for me, it had to based on where God was calling me. In earnest, I began to research the Catholic faith, and this would lead me to discover the Catholic Church had much more to offer than I had ever imagined.

My Faith on Fire

In my baptism, I received sanctifying grace. Fr. Brian Thomas Becket Mullady describes grace as:

> a disposition or quality of being—a true interior change— by which we become a new creation and in which we partake of the divine nature itself. Man raised up by grace is called a new creation because as God created something from nothing in the first creation, he introduces something brand-new—grace—into our souls without prior merit. Man becomes a new creation not as something different than a being having a human soul and body, but as a being able to act perfectly to fulfill the purpose of that soul's creation. The term *habit* is a good one for this because it simply means a new kind of existing with new possibility of acting: to know as God knows and love as God loves. We do not become God, but we act as he does.[2]

As I began taking advantage of as many graces as God offered and I could handle, which to be honest was thimble-sized amounts at first, my practice of faith became a habit, and in turn my openness to allowing him into more areas of my life expanded exponentially. Now, my soul was ready for more abundant graces, which I became all the more prepared to receive when I participated in the Church's many devotions (including the plethora of sacramentals) I'd soon discover.

These graces, this awareness of God in all places and every aspect of my life, would spread from Sundays and special occasion connections to Christ to real, tangible experiences amid ordinary circumstances. No one would ever have convinced me in December of 2005 that the accelerating momentum of experiencing faith in my life would stem from an invitation to Bible study, but it did. Once I began making regular scripture reading part of my prayer routine, doors in my soul I didn't even know existed began to creak open. This little snowball of faith continued on its merry way, accumulating more and more bits of grace as I learned about the Church's plethora of devotions, especially sacramentals. The simple practice of reading the Word of God propped open the doors of courage, obedience, and trust I needed even to consider what at the time felt like God's crazy plan for our family to adopt from China.

Scripture as Sacramental

We've already discussed that sacramentals are reminders, symbols, and preparation of the soul for the grace God offers us. This is my abridged definition of grace: the undeserved yet freely given gift of God's Holy Spirit within us. That profound movement of the Spirit helps us believe, choose good, courageously share our faith with others, and so much more. And what could be a more significant reminder of God's promises than his Word? We do not have to guess how God communicates or how he sounds; we can merely open the words of the precious document that is the Bible to be enlightened and blessed.

John's contributions to the scriptures inspired me not only to read more but also to believe and rely on the Word of God as a spiritual compass. Additionally, St. Paul teaches us that the scriptures are good for teaching and so much more. Our faith is not based only on scripture, however; we are also blessed with tradition. My encounters with the different sacramentals shared in this book led me to make one of the most significant decisions of my life: to travel to China and add a sweet little three-year-old child to our family. Although my baptism infused me with sanctifying grace and began my Christian journey, for a decision this significant, discovering the scriptures, establishing a relationship with Jesus, and leaning into all the grace God had to offer were crucial steps to move me forward.

Teaching Scripture without Words: St. John

Teaching the Word of God to somebody who has not yet developed language—well, I thought that would be the most daunting task of passing along my faith to my daughter. But I realized that the Church had long found ways to share the Good News with those who could not read and in some cases could not understand.

The scriptures include teachings, parables, explanations, and nuances buried within the words, making them at times tricky for anyone. We certainly weren't looking to make Faithy a scripture scholar; however, this aspect of the faith was critical because it was how I came to know Christ before adopting her. My faith journey deeper into the heart of Jesus could be described as a double reversion. The initial reorientation toward Christ came in 1991, when Kevin and I returned to Mass, however, it wouldn't be until 2005, and the study of scripture that I fell in love with Jesus. I knew from my own experience being led back to Jesus from a very lukewarm, perfunctory faith how much the Word of God can transform a heart. I had attended Mass back in the 1990s as a preventative measure—you know, if this Jesus thing is real, I wanted to be able to show perfect attendance at the pearly gates—so my heart was rarely in the liturgy. It was once I began to study God's Word that I made that successful journey from head to heart, and I longed for my baby girl to experience the same joy of knowing God in such an intimate way through his words.

The methods I used with my boys—Bible study for children, Vacation Bible School, youth group, Christian concerts, and even the *VeggieTales* cartoons—were avenues that wouldn't work for her, at least not at first. Faithy's input had to be visual, which led me to picture Bibles and stained glass windows. With the windows, I was relying on the wisdom of the cloud of witnesses in the Church before me who created stained glass windows for passing on the faith to those who could not read. Showing Faithy the beauty of the Church was how I started to teach her about God and so much more.

Through the wonders of the internet, we traveled across the globe and peered into churches, museums, and shrines without ever leaving our home. Long before quarantines made this the only way to travel, it was mostly our pocketbook that kept us field tripping from the comfort of our couch, though we did visit local shrines and churches. I think sometimes we forget we can pilgrimage right in our backyards.

As Catholics, we hear the Word of God weekly at Mass from sacred scripture. (I was almost forty years old before I learned that the Mass readings were scripture; I don't know how I missed that, and I'm a little embarrassed to admit it. In my immature faith, I guess I figured the bishops were outstanding writers.) We must stay connected to the Word of God after we leave Church on Sunday. The Mass is where we encounter God in the most profound way we ever will in our lives; why would we not want to continue that intimacy beyond the church walls and bring it into our homes, the domestic church.

Equipping Us for Good Works

One lesson I pray as Faithy matures, and is better able to understand the written word, that I can guide her in using the scriptures to discern God's will in her life. For years, I remember lamenting at struggling to hear God's voice, especially when faced with making decisions. St. Paul's words in 2 Timothy clued me into the missing piece of my listening for God puzzle, "All scripture is inspired by God and profitable for teaching, for reproof, for correction, and for training in righteousness, that the man of God may be complete, equipped for every good work" (3:16–17). Scripture holds every answer, because it is the inspired words of the One who knows all, sees all, and whose will is for good—including my good!

I probably should not admit this in writing, but sometimes when interpreting the homily for Faithy, I might interject some motherly advice on how the readings are personally related to what is going on in her life. While most families might use the car ride home to discuss such things, parents of deaf kids have to be a little more creative (and safe, both hands on the wheel, right!) We have also taken to using graphic, comic strip style, books about the saints and the scriptures to help her begin to learn the stories so as to eventually transpose the virtues she reads about into her own decision making. Faithy has proved to me that hearing God's voice does not require functioning ears, but a heart tuned to the Spirit's omnipotent frequency.

St. John the Evangelist

John was the son of Zebedee and Salome, and the brother of James the Greater. Tradition estimates his birth to be AD 15, which would make him only eighteen years of age when Jesus began his public ministry. He was a fisherman working alongside his father and brother; tradition holds that they may have been partners with Simon Peter and his brother, Andrew. The day John and the others met Jesus, as told in the Gospels, their hard work had not been paying off. They toiled all night, but no fish filled their nets. Jesus entered the boat of Simon, instructed them to try something different—cast their nets to the other side—and suddenly their nets were overflowing to the point of breaking. While they were still reeling from the catch, Jesus astonished them further by calling them to be his disciples, to leave everything and follow him. Immediately, they did just that.

St. John the Evangelist, known also as St. John the Apostle to differentiate him from St. John the Baptist, in addition to writing one of the four Gospels, is credited with the writing of Revelation and two epistles. He is the only apostle not martyred, although the exact date and circumstances of his death are not certain. Tradition relates that he was cast into a cauldron of boiling oil by order of Emperor Domitian but came forth unhurt and was banished to the island of Patmos for a year. He lived to an extreme old age, surviving all his fellow apostles, and died in Ephesus about the year 100.

The Church celebrates his feast day on December 27, ironically in the season of Christmas although he is the only Gospel writer not to include a narrative on the Nativity of the Lord. Another interesting fact to note: John, the only apostle to remain with Jesus throughout his Passion and death, was also the only one not martyred. Perhaps a grace for his loyalty and kindness toward Mary? We'll never know this side of heaven, but it is something worthy of pondering.

The Bible as a Sacramental

> In the beginning was the Word, and the Word was with God, and the Word was God. He was with God in the beginning. Through him all things were made; without him nothing was made that has been made.
>
> —*John 1:1-3*

Scripture serves as means of grace in the Christian life; as with all sacramentals, merely possessing a Bible does not make us holy. It is our use of the item with a desire to grow in holiness that increases our readiness and disposes us to receive the grace God has for us. Sanctifying grace stays in the soul, but actual grace is transient. It acts on the soul from the outside, animating the heart and the head to cooperate to maintain sanctifying grace. Being a disciple, following God's way when the world pulls in the opposite direction, is hard work and, thanks to free will, requires some effort on our part. God never makes his holy goals impossible for us; he is love himself after all (see 1 John 4:8). Time spent with the scriptures creates encounters with the Word of God—with Jesus, who is the Word made flesh. These encounters are avenues of grace. They bless us, strengthen our faith, and open our hearts to the movement of grace in our lives. While this is not Church doctrine, out of all the sacramentals and devotions shared in this book, time with the Bible—regular scripture reading and study—is in my opinion the most foundational and profound avenue to a life of grace.

Adopting a More Tangible Faith

Growing in Grace with Scripture

> Blessed be the God and Father of our Lord Jesus Christ,
> who has blessed us in Christ with every spiritual blessing
> in the heavens, as he chose us in him, before the founda-
> tion of the world, to be holy and without blemish before
> him. In love he destined us for adoption to himself through
> Jesus Christ, in accord with the favor of his will, for the
> praise of the glory of his grace that he granted us in the
> beloved. (Eph 1:3–6, NABRE)

In the Bible, the faithful discover their inheritance as adopted sons and daughters. We are provided the perfect model in Jesus, who teaches, corrects, encourages, and guides all souls toward heaven. Our hope of heaven—the eternal life that only Jesus can offer—instills a joy that no circumstance in this life can shake. In the scriptures, we also encounter our Blessed Mother, who holds the unique role of daughter of the Father, mother of the Son, and spouse of the Holy Spirit. Filled with grace, she intercedes for us and guides us in the way of joy.

Joy, one of God's spiritual blessings, shines far beyond the absence of worldly troubles. It is the knowledge of God's unfathomable, unbreakable love for us; the promise of God, our Father, to never abandon or forsake his children. Furthermore, there is a place in our Father's house for us as coheirs, a place Jesus has gone ahead to prepare for us and will come back to bring us to (see John 14). Jesus is the way to the Father. Mary pondered in her heart every word that came from the mouth of God. Jesus said, "Let not your hearts be troubled; believe in God, believe also in me" (Jn 14:1). When we seek, knock, and ask for consolation through the scriptures, especially if we make this a daily practice, we will develop, like Mary, a heart that nothing can disturb.

Uncovering Grace

1. What encounters with Mary, a saint, or people in your life have drawn you closer to Jesus? Did they introduce you to a particular

devotion in the Catholic faith that you continue to practice? Have you ever participated in a small-group book club (or Bible study)? Did you find sharing your favorite traditions, devotions, or discoveries of faith advantageous in strengthening your own faith?

2. How familiar are you with the scriptures? Do you have a favorite book, verse, or author in the Bible? In what ways can you integrate the scriptures into your regular prayer practices?

3. Does your life include any "I could never do that" moments? How did the practice of your faith influence your forging forward with the mission? As you go forward, how can you incorporate the scriptures in discerning God's will in your life?

Grace-Building Activities

- Annotate your Bible. The art of reading scripture through lectio divina ("divine reading") is a beautiful, long-held tradition (see appendix for instructions). What I am going to suggest may scandalize you, but hear me out. Get yourself a nice set of colored, no-bleed-through gel pens, highlighters, and sticky notes. You, my friend, are going to embrace the Bible as never before. As you read these divinely inspired words, write (*yes, in your Bible*) how they inspire you—underline words that speak to your heart at that moment, star verses that convict as well as encourage, and plop in a colorful sticky tab to remind you to come back and look at a passage again later. If you are new to the Bible, purchase a set of chapter tabs or create your own. My first Bible received back in eighth grade was tabbed with scotch tape and a sharpie! Your Bible is yours, and it is not sacrilege to genuinely engage with the words and emotions stirred as you read it. The markings help you remember what God, through the Holy Spirit, is saying to you. They can be crucial in times of difficulty or spiritual dryness in helping you recall Jesus's promises. Don't be shy; get on in there and experience the Bible as never before!

- Create your own stained glass windows to tell scripture stories. You can use colored construction paper: draw the outlines of your windows with a black marker; glue gray, gold, or black yarn along the lines for a 3D effect; and then fill in the spaces with torn or cut-out shapes to create the stained glass effect. Other creative ways to create homemade windows include decoupaging tissue paper on wax paper with watery glue; your "window" can then be hung in an actual window for light to penetrate through as it does in the church. To appreciate the true brilliance of a stained glass window, one must be inside the church, especially when the light of the sun streams through from the other side. While you can catch of glimpse of the story the window tells from outside, it is not fully illuminated until you have entered into the sanctuary of the church.

- Choose a family verse. Paint on a board or use letter stickers and post in your home a Bible verse that tells a story about who you are as a family. A friend of mine would make "life verse" plaques for milestone birthdays. She would pay attention during Bible study to see if you were drawn to a particular verse. At that time, I really loved Galatians 2:20 ("It is no longer I who live, but Christ who lives in me"), and if she had asked me then which one I'd want on the plaque, that is what I would have chosen. However, during the adoption of my daughter, she saw each week that my stories were leaning toward my incredible trust in the Lord, so on my fortieth birthday she handed me a plaque that read "Trust in the Lord with all your heart, and lean not on your own understanding" (Prv 3:5 [NIV]).

- During Advent, create a Jesse Tree. You can place homemade ornaments on a small tree, branch, dowel, or another creative structure your family finds to display them. The ornaments bring us through salvation history and are a simple, visual way to teach the Old Testament prophecy about Jesus as well as represent the ancient ancestors in the lineage of Jesus (making this activity useful for chapter 9). We used the Mosaic Jesse Tree template from Sara Estabrooks's website (ToJesusSincerely.com). Each set includes twenty-five cardstock ornaments and a 6×9 booklet with scriptures, reflections, and prayers for each day. There are many different Jesse Tree kit options available including quilting or felting patterns found on Jen Frost's FaithandFabricDesign.com.

8

Someone to Look Up To

St. Juan Diego
and Sacred Images

> When we show reverence to representations of Jesus
> Christ, we do not worship paint laid on wood—we
> worship the invisible God, in spirit and in truth.
> —*St. Germanus of Constantinople*

Never Too Old for Mission

At fifty-seven, Juan Diego, the Mexican peasant to whom the sacred
image of Our Lady of Guadalupe was entrusted, thought his life's work
was winding down. Instead, while simply going about his everyday
life, trying to grow in faithfulness by attending Mass and caring for
his family, he would accomplish the most remarkable thing of his life.
There was something in his heart such that Mother Mary knew he was
the one she could bring her vital mission to, that he'd be the one to say
yes and see it through.

At forty, I believed my vocation of motherhood to be entering a
new phase of coasting, not additional responsibilities that pushed me
far out of my comfort zone. Yet after two premature births and two
miscarriages, one of which nearly cost me my life from complications,
here I was discerning in prayer that we were being nudged to adopt.
And not just any adoption, but the adoption of a special needs child,
who currently lived in a communist country literally half a world

away. With all my anxieties and self-doubts, I kept trying to avoid the Spirit's nudges and hide.

See, the interesting thing is God doesn't force us to cooperate with his graces; that is for us to decide. However, he does promise that he will never ask the impossible (see Matthew 19:26) and that he will be with us until the end of time (see Matthew 28:20). He will bestow every grace and blessing necessary, but we must still cooperate due to our free will. And that's where we stood at Mass on a fateful Sunday in February 2006, praying and trying to determine if what the Spirit had sparked in our hearts—to adopt a child from China—was of God or if we'd gone and lost our minds.

The deacon began the Prayers of the Faithful. My mind wandered as I begged for clarity, and prayed, *Lord, if this is truly what you want, I will go, but I need to be sure because I am scared, insecure as to my abilities, and, well, broke.* Just as my attention returned to the deacon's voice, I heard, "And may all the orphans of the world find good homes." Not sure Jesus could have been any clearer with that perfectly timed *godcidence*!

Sacred Images, Family Photos

If you walk down the hallway of my family's home, you are flanked on each side by images of all those we love and have loved: grandparents, aunts and uncles, nieces and nephews, friends—all the people who bless our lives and who, on occasion, we've needed to reach out to for help. Sacred images that adorn my house serve a similar purpose—to remind me of all those in my heavenly family who have blessed my life and, on many occasions, come to my aid and assistance! Seeing their faces helps me feel connected, even though we've never met.

One image in the hallway is of my daughter's sponsored friend in the Philippines; we chose this child because she shares Faithy's birthday, a date selected at the time of her abandonment to which we've sought to give meaning for her. Just as the many prayers we exchange with our saint posse have made them part of our family, this child we've never met has indeed become part of our family through years of correspondence. Although we are the ones giving her assistance, she has blessed us in innumerable ways.

Faithy came to us with nothing. She has no photos from her family of origin or even from her foster family, with whom she spent nearly four years of her life. One of the things we were taught in our preparation for the adoption was how to help our child deal with feelings of abandonment. Paramount for me was helping her embrace and believe in God's promise that "I will never fail you nor forsake you" (Heb 13:5). Regardless of what the world has to offer, what it gives or takes away, her Father in heaven will always be a steadfast fixture in her life.

Our Catholic faith provided us an incredible opportunity to introduce her to the heavenly family her baptism made her a part of, which nothing can separate her from. A whole cloud of witnesses (see Hebrews 12:1), a saint posse, became her heavenly family. Of course, our earthly family has embraced her without reservation, but given that two earthly families had separated from her before she reached ours, we wanted to assure her that a family exists for her that she can trust and rely on. A family of faith for Faithy—what could be more fitting! We spent time at the Daughters of St. Paul bookstore choosing prayer cards with saints that meant something to our family—St. Francis de Sales (patron of the deaf), St. Michael the Archangel, St. Thérèse, and Padre Pio, to name just a few. I punched a heart-shaped hole in the corner of each laminated card, put a blue (her favorite color) metal carabiner clip, and we brought this with us for car rides and to occupy her in Mass (before she and I understood enough sign language for me to interpret it). We added to her wall an image of the Blessed Mother and a crucifix with Jesus, his hands in the "I love you" ASL sign. We gave her an adorable St. Thérèse of Lisieux doll and Padre Pio, Our Lady of China, and St. Nicholas figurines to keep her company at night and help make these people real in her life.

The Many Ways We Learn

For my daughter's first Christmas, we purchased the cutest Fisher-Price nativity playset. The little figurines—saint statues, if you will—gave us a playful way to introduce Jesus, Mary, and Joseph into her life, as well as the awesomeness of angels. Although, given her penchant for speaking to her guardian angel, I have a feeling she was already well acquainted with angels before she ever received that plastic one!

As a former educator, I knew that people learn in three primary modalities—kinesthetic, auditory, and visual. Kinesthetic learning takes place while a person is in the act of physically doing something, such as riding a bike or manipulating adorable, pint-sized Holy Family figurines! Auditory and visual learning are self-explanatory, and because in Faithy's case, one of those—hearing the lessons to learn—is not an option, that meant a greater reliance on the other two. As you've probably already noticed, we did our best to provide as much visual input into teaching the faith as possible.

It is nice when we can bring in activities such as praying the Rosary with her crocheted roses, strolling around a shrine, or creating arts and crafts that fortify the devotions, traditions, and rudimentary theology we are trying to transmit. As a bonus to all of this, I have garnered a more profound understanding, appreciation, and passion for my Catholic faith in participating in these activities. Fun fact: how we learned best as children remains our learning style throughout our lives, and when we can incorporate two or more of the modalities into what we are studying, we discover even more about the subject. And who doesn't want to learn as much as possible about God? Sure, he is unfathomable, but there is still so much we can uncover!

Tucking Prayers

In an address to the people of the Philippines on January 16, 2015, Pope Francis shared, "I have great love for Saint Joseph, because he is a man of silence and strength. On my table I have an image of Saint Joseph sleeping. Even when he is asleep, he is taking care of the Church!" During the Year of St. Joseph, Pope Francis advised people to tuck a note, a prayer request, under the image of the saint for help whenever they have a problem. The image of the sleeping Joseph comes from the Gospel accounts of the Angel of the Lord appearing four times to Joseph in his dreams to provide him counsel in times of uncertainty. The first occurred when he learned of Mary's conception of the infant and tried to discern how to protect her reputation. Trusting in the truth of the angel's words—"Joseph, son of David, do not be afraid to take Mary your wife, for that which is conceived in her is of the Holy Spirit" (Mt 1:20)—Joseph woke and did as instructed. Joseph had another angelic dream when Herod, seeking to destroy this newborn king, began slaughtering male babies in Bethlehem; he again followed the guidance of the angel of the Lord, this time fleeing with his little holy family to Egypt to keep them safe (see Matthew 2:13–18).

Later, in that same address in the Philippines, Pope Francis added, "But like Saint Joseph, once we have heard God's voice, we must rise from our slumber; we must get up and act." Pope Francis said on that occasion that faith does not distance us from the world; on the contrary, it brings us closer. For that reason, St. Joseph is a model father for the Christian family. He overcame the difficulties of life because he rested with God.[1]

While our family does not possess a sleeping Joseph statue, we do have a small alabaster depiction of St. Joseph, lily and carpenter square in one hand, baby Jesus in the other. I have tucked many a prayer under his feet for his intercession while I rest from this concern. House woes, financial burdens, prodigal children—all have been and remain tucked in his loving care. Showing Faithy how to write down her prayers, concerns, even hopes and dreams, and tuck them in the loving care of one of her saint friends has provided yet another opportunity to teach her about intercessory prayer and how our faith can give us peace and rest.

Jesus invites all who are burdened and weary to yoke ourselves to him and there find comfort and rest (see Matthew 11:28–30). The holy men and women who have gone before us, especially his Blessed Mother and holy foster father, Joseph, are part of that plan for carrying our burdens. The Communion of Saints, whose images we can surround ourselves with, do more than brighten a decor; they provide visual reminders we are loved and covered continually in the prayers of the faithful, both living and dead. Then, once we've placed our prayers, we must—like Joseph—trust, rise, and do what we can in the matters before us. Whether that means boarding a plane to China to bring home a toddler who is deaf, getting up and driving to work each day, or caring for a sick relative, if we are breathing, God has great plans for us. Thankfully, we can all rest with our heavenly prayer brigade behind us.

Faithy, Our Lady, and Lessons
in Intercessory Prayer

Our pew is directly before a life-size image of Our Lady of Guadalupe next to a candle stand with jars of long white candles you can
light for personal intentions. Our Lady of Guadalupe has long been
one of my favorites. What image could be more tangible evidence of
the heavenly reality of Mary's existence? A little divine intervention
put the image and the candles together where Faithy would see them
every week, providing the perfect opportunity to teach her another
way to pray for others. Lighting candles for our family, friends, and
even strangers, and then kneeling before the Blessed Sacrament and
the multiple powerful and prominent images and statues our parish
is blessed to have was a kinetic and visual experience that even at a
very young age she could begin to grasp.

We have adoration at our parish on First Fridays in the church,
where I could bring her to pray before the image of Our Lady of Guadalupe on the side of the altar, Jesus in the monstrance, and the image
of Divine Mercy that flanks the other side of our altar. Our altar also
has a restored relief of the Last Supper. The images in our parish, as
in all churches, are not there merely for decoration but serve a great
purpose—to point our hearts heavenward. Sometimes I think we can
become blind to them. My daughter, who notices things I may never
see, has taught me to open my eyes more widely to take in the world
around me with curiosity and a heart to learn. She's always pointing
out little details I could so easily overlook in the bustle of my life. It
is a nice change of pace; since I get to be her ears so often, I love that
she gets to be my keener sight—which the older I get, the more I need!

Sacred Space and Time at Home

I am blessed to be one of the hosts of the CatholicMom.com *Momcast*
podcast. A few months ago, Danielle Bean and I did an episode on
sanctifying our homes. Danielle shared this tip for creating a prayer
space, especially if you don't have the luxury of keeping a prayer corner
up all the time. She puts special items such as an image of the Blessed
Mother, a Bible, a candle, and a small crucifix in a drawer and pulls
them out for her prayer time—not only does this bless her prayer

time, but an unexpected benefit is that it became a visual way for her family to recognize this sacred time. When my kids were younger, the rule during Mom's prayer time—to be followed unless someone was bleeding or the house was on fire—was to come back later with their questions. Scheduled or dedicated prayer time is such a fabulous way of setting this time apart from the rest of your day and, if you are able, from the rest of your home. In making your prayer time sacred, you show your children where you place God in your life.

In chapter 4, I mentioned my friend's mother, Mrs. Profetty, who gave me the St. Thérèse novena card. She had set a comfortable chair and small side table in the corner of their living room. I remember the table overflowing with prayer cards, spiritual reading, and a Bible, topped with her rosary beads tucked carefully in an embroidered pouch. You knew what priority she placed on her relationship with Christ, not only by the quaint prayer corner but also by the prints throughout her home of the Sacred Heart of Jesus and the Immaculate Heart of Mary. The family also painted life-sized statues of the saints for local churches. Funny story about these statues: the family failed to inform me of this volunteer activity tucked safely in their basement, and you should have heard me scream the first time I turned the corner and unexpectedly "met" St. Anthony face-to-face!

It is not lost on me that many of the ways I found to teach or share the faith with my daughter, including teaching her about intercessory prayer, came from praying to the saints for intercession. Just like the police, I need to call for backup. Isn't that what, in essence, intercessory prayer is—calling in the cavalry? The saints have our backs, spiritually speaking. And many of the early lessons Faithy picked up about the faith came from mimicking my behavior. I am sure that the first time she and I knelt before the image of Our Lady of Guadalupe to pray, she was clueless about what was happening. Yet my daughter copied my prayer posture precisely. She knelt, leaning on the altar rail, hands pressed flat together, with eyes lifted to Mary. One way we learn from the saints is by copying their journey to heaven and interactions with Christ.

St. Juan Diego

Juan Diego Cuauhtlatoatzin, first known as Cuauhtlatohuac ("The Eagle Who Speaks"), was born in 1474 in Mexico. One of the Chichimeca people, he was baptized around 1524 by Friar Peter da Gand, an early Franciscan missionary.

On December 9, 1531, when Juan Diego was on his way to religious education and morning Mass at the Franciscan mission, the Blessed Mother appeared to him on Tepeyac Hill, in what is now the outskirts of Mexico City. She asked him to go to the bishop and to request in her name that a shrine be built at Tepeyac, where she promised to pour out her grace upon those who invoked her. Bishop Juan de Zumarrága, who did not believe Juan Diego, asked for a sign to prove that the apparition was true. Juan and our Blessed Mother had two other encounters before this one on December 12, when she intercepted Juan Diego as he tried to avoid his appointment with her in order to retrieve a priest to anoint his sick uncle. She then spoke these words of comfort to him, "Am I not here, I, who am your Mother? Are you not under my shadow and protection? Am I not the source of your joy? Are you not in the hollow of my mantle, in the crossing of my arms? Do you need anything more? Let nothing else worry you, disturb you." Then, the Blessed Mother instructed him to climb the hill and to pick the flowers that he would find in bloom there. He obeyed, and although it was wintertime, he found roses flowering. He gathered the flowers and took them to Our Lady, who carefully placed them in his tilma (cloak) and told him to take them to the bishop as "proof." When he opened his tilma for the bishop, the flowers fell on the ground, and there remained impressed on the tilma, in place of the flowers, an image of the Blessed Mother, the apparition at Tepeyac.

Because he trusted in the Blessed Mother and followed through with his mission, even at the age of fifty-seven, Juan's brave actions aided in the conversion of millions of people, and the tilma continues to draw people to Mary and her Son today.[2]

Sacred Images

Every genuine art form in its own way is a path to
the inmost reality of man and of the world. It is
therefore a wholly valid approach to the realm of
faith, which gives human experience its ultimate
meaning. That is why the Gospel fullness of truth
was bound from the beginning to stir the interest
of artists, who by their very nature are alert to every
"epiphany" of the inner beauty of things.

—Pope John Paul II to Artists

The Second Council of Nicaea in 787 emphatically encouraged the
veneration of the images of the saints, whether "depicted in mosaic
or any other suitable material, and exposed in the holy churches of
God, on their furnishings, vestments, on their walls, as well as in the
homes of the faithful and in the streets, be they images of Our Lord
God and Saviour Jesus Christ, or of Our Immaculate Lady, the holy
Mother of God, or of the Angels, the Saints and the just."

Furthermore, the reverence of sacred images, whether paint-
ings, statues, bas-reliefs, or other representations, was deemed a
valuable aspect of popular piety, to be done both in churches and
in homes. These images not only remind us of the holy men and
women who have come before us but also help direct and focus
our prayers.[3]

Adopting a More Tangible Faith

Growing in Grace with Scripture

Then [Jesus] returned from the region of Tyre, and went
through Sidon to the Sea of Galilee, through the region
of the Decap'olis. And they brought to him a man who
was deaf and had an impediment in his speech; and they

besought him to lay his hand upon him. And taking him
aside from the multitude privately, he put his fingers into
his ears, and he spat and touched his tongue; and looking
up to heaven, he sighed, and said to him, "Eph'phatha," that
is, "Be opened." And his ears were opened, his tongue was
released, and he spoke plainly. And he charged them to tell
no one; but the more he charged them, the more zealously
they proclaimed it. And they were astonished beyond measure, saying, "He has done all things well; he even makes
the deaf hear and the dumb speak." (Mk 7:31–37)

A few months after my daughter arrived home with us, I confided
to my husband that I had tried to perform the same miracle on her
after reading this passage in Mark. My husband burst into laughter;
when he finally regained his composure, he shared he'd done the same
thing! It is not that we were trying to fix Faithy's deafness. Of course,
we love her just the way she is and trust in God's plan for her life, that
she's at peace with being deaf is evident by interminable joy. But as a
parent, you can't help but be acutely aware that possessing the ability
to hear in a hearing world wouldn't necessarily be a bad thing for
Faithy. Her ears did not open from our prayers or our gross wet fingers (coincidentally, we both chose not to touch her tongue with our
spit but instead took our chance with the ear). The lack of a miracle,
however, did not shake our faith—for reasons only God knows, this
was not his will for her. Oh, and the look on her face was priceless!

What we have learned over the years raising our daughter is that
you do not need ears that hear to be a faithful disciple. Being open to
Christ working in your life requires humility, surrender, and obedience
to accept your life with joy instead of constantly chasing dreams God
never intended for you to dream. Discernment of the life God wills
for you, the one that leads you to heaven, begins with prayer. If you
struggle to make prayer part of your daily routine, a well-placed sacred
image might be the perfect reminder. An icon on your desk, a tiny
statue on your bureau, even a magnet on the fridge can help remind
you to be open to Christ working in your life.

Uncovering Grace

1. Do you have sacred images displayed in your home? Which ones do you feel most connected to? What do you hope people visiting your home will learn about you and your faith from the holy art they see there?
2. What missions has God sent you on? Do you currently feel a nudge from the Holy Spirit to evangelize, serve, or in some way accomplish something that would glorify God? What would you need to assure you that the nudge is from the Spirit? How could you begin today to move toward living this call?
3. In what ways do you need to be opened to see the plans God has for you? When you get overwhelmed or worried, do you try to skirt around coming to God (all of heaven really—Mary, angels, and saints) in prayer? Can you think of a few places to stash a sacred image, statue, or icon to keep your daily prayer life on course?

Grace-Building Activities

- Create a family shrine or prayer table. Aunt Louise, my godmother, had a little table with a candle she lit every time a loved one was traveling or in need of special prayer. The shrine also included images of our Blessed Mother, Jesus, and loved ones who had passed away. She kept her rosary beads, some prayer cards, and a little jar of holy water on the table as well. It was the place she retired to each day for her prayer time. What would such a table look like in your home?
- Make your own icon. You can find instructions online or take a course. My parish followed the step-by-step, eight-day (though we set it up for eight weeks), self-guided contemplative retreat found in iconographer Joseph Malham's book *Drawing Closer to Christ* (Ave Maria Press, 2017). This book uses the ancient icon Christ Pantocrator as its pattern. As you read through the retreat, you learn how to enter into the process of tracing the icon onto the wood, applying gold leafing to the halo around Christ's head, and blending the paint to create beautiful colors that radiate holiness.

The book provides a list of supplies needed for each stage and step-by-step directions with detailed photographs!

- Write a prayer request, and tuck it under a saint statue in your home. Invite your family to write prayer requests as well. These can remain secret, though prayers are not like birthday wishes that we believe we have to keep to ourselves or they won't come true. Select a statue in your home—it does not have to be a sleeping St. Joseph, nor do all prayers need to all go under the same saint's feet. Say a prayer, either out loud or to yourself, invoking the heavenly aid of the saint for your petition, and then gently tuck the note into the care of the saint. Should your prayer be answered, say a prayer of thanksgiving, remove the prayer, and add a new one. Remember that all prayer is answered; sometimes the answer is not yes but no (because it is not part of God's will for you) or not yet. But you can rest assured that your prayers will be answered.

9

Staying Connected to Church

St. Bernadette Soubirous, Holy Water, Incense, and Candles

Thus the little domestic Church, like the greater Church, needs to be constantly and intensely evangelized: hence its duty regarding permanent education in the faith. . . . "The family, like the Church, ought to be a place where the Gospel is transmitted and from which the Gospel radiates." . . . [T]he future of evangelization depends in great part on the Church of the home.

—*St. John Paul II*

A Beacon of Hope in China

On our last Sunday in China, we and the other Catholic family who traveled with us went looking for a Catholic Mass with our newly adopted little girls. We realized it was a bit of a needle-in-a-haystack situation, but I had seen a church on one of our strolls around Guangzhou, drawn by its delicate, teeny, faded-blue statue of the Blessed Mother tucked in an arched alcove in the front facade. I was optimistic, maybe more hopeful than I should have been, that we would be able to attend Mass that morning. When we arrived for Mass at the time the translator had instructed us to, we found no people, only steel bars and a padlock preventing us from even peeking inside of this precious little church nestled in the middle of China.

Not to be defeated, we returned to the other family's hotel room to at least spend time in prayer together. I had the *Magnificat* missal with the daily Mass readings with me. After listening to the readings, we decided to take a few minutes to share where we had experienced the presence of God throughout the adoption experience, especially during our time in China.

I went first and shared what I had written on my blog about God's patience waiting for me to return his love, and that I was grateful for my daughter and was prepared to do the same for her until she was ready to choose to receive my love. Everyone on the trip knew Faithy resisted every attempt for me to bond with her. She had, until this point, completely rejected me. She wouldn't allow me to get anywhere near her, and I struggled to shake the memory of her meltdown in the hotel in Wuhan when she and had I spent a few hours alone while Kevin and the translator went to Walmart (yes, even in China, we needed a trip to Walmart!). I'll never forget the look on Faithy's face the minute the door closed behind them; she burst into tears and cried so hard that she threw up all over me. Always optimistic, I did see the good of our first solo encounter—it was when I knew for sure I was her mother because you're not genuinely inaugurated as a parent until you have a child's bodily fluids on you.

Just as I finished my sharing, as if on cue, Faithy reached out to me from her stroller! (I had been trying to take her out since we had arrived, but she had fussed at me and refused to allow it. Faithy is so headstrong—an admirable quality unless you are trying to get her to do something.) First, she hugged me; then she lifted her hands for me to get her out. It was such a gift from God, a beacon of hope, one of those amazing moments I once heard referred to as "kisses from the King." As we wiped tears from our eyes, we realized Faithy was just using me as a means to be freed from her stroller prison. Our tears quickly changed to laughter, but it was still a glimmer that we were turning a corner because she hadn't looked to Dad but to me as her ticket to freedom.

As we were leaving for dinner shortly after this unforgettable moment, I told Kevin that perhaps God was allowing this to be so hard because he knew that now I'd relish every moment and not take one for granted. With my boys, I felt like life was so hectic—trying to finish school, work, care for the house, etc.—that maybe I missed some kisses the King had sent because I was too busy to notice. In this situation, I was much more appreciative and aware of working so hard for every smile, kiss, connection. I am grateful that God has given me so many beams of light in the darkness and the wherewithal not to miss any of them!

The Breakthrough

It would be another Sunday, about three weeks later, when I'd see the fruit of my prayers, patience, and persistence, and the outpouring of God's grace come together in the miracle I'd been waiting for. We were back home, with me sitting in the family room with my son Adam on my lap and Faithy tucked comfortably in the chair with her new dad. We were discussing Kevin's return to work the next day. Kevin had major concerns about my being alone with Faithy for the first time since her big meltdown in Wuhan. He was stressed, wondering if he should extend his paternity leave.

I reassured him that as former daycare provider and preschool teacher, I'd spent many a morning with hysterical children at the door waiting for their parents to come back and for me to be gone! I reminded him of how many promises God had already fulfilled. He'd brought us to this incredible mission, empowered us with the grace to accept it, and provided in every possible way, from finding her to making it work financially; he'd certainly not abandon us now. "Trust he has a plan, and it is always for good," I said.

Just as I was finishing these words, with my son cuddled all the deeper into my embrace, Faithy suddenly tilted her head and looked enviously across the room. She struggled off her dad's lap, waddled across the room as quickly as her weak-muscle-toned legs could take her, arrived at my chair, pushed her brother off my lap, and took his place. This time, the tears turned into laughter out of joy, for we had just witnessed our surrender to God's will bring the result we had been waiting for. Just as I finally accepted God as my Father, recognizing he is genuinely trustworthy, faithful, kind, and loving—so much more than just a provider of my needs—something within Faithy finally recognized that same connection to me. We've been the best of friends ever since that moment! If you ask her who her favorite in the family is, she quickly, albeit coyly, signs, "Mom."

Bringing the Church Home

Since we are created in God's likeness and image, it doesn't seem a far reach to assume that he intended for us to use all the senses he gave us to communicate and connect with him—more avenues for us to take full advantage of the abundant grace he has for us. The Mass is the highest and most perfect form of prayer, where all our senses are activated: We see what happens on the altar. We hear the music and the Word of God. We touch and can taste the Body, Blood, soul, and divinity of Our Lord Jesus Christ in the Eucharist. We reach out and feel the hands of our neighbors as we give the Sign of Peace (as long as we're not in the middle of a pandemic). We inhale the fragrant smell of incense and perhaps catch faint whiffs of the burning candles. Mass—with the standing, sitting, kneeling, genuflecting, handshaking, head bowing, Sign of the Cross making, and more—is truly a full-body experience, replete with majesty and meaning.

Jesus, who is incarnate and like us in every way but sin (see Hebrews 4:15), experienced the world in his human nature, through his senses. Even though my daughter's sense of hearing is impaired, I do not doubt that her other senses make up for that in ways I will never fully understand, including how she comprehends different aspects of our Catholic faith. Witnessing my daughter engage with the graces dispensed through the sacraments, especially the Mass, I've learned new ways to cooperate with, connect to, and receive the gifts of God's grace through all my senses. But the Mass is not meant to be a one-hour experience of God. We can bring home those experiences to our "domestic churches"—in other words, how we live our faith within our homes, seeing our families as a little church. We can live the grace of the sacraments every day in our lives through sacramentals.

Jesus is the best teacher, and he uses sacramental language and signs to communicate to us and place the grace of eternal life within our souls. He calls us to share in his divine life. When we are properly disposed to receive it, sacramentals can be extensions of that grace, working within our human nature. Again, being the best teacher, he wants us to be praying without ceasing, abiding in his love—it's a 24/7 proposition, and he holds back nothing. God does not complicate things or purposefully make things too difficult to be accomplished. Even if we find it impossible, for as we see in Mark's gospel: "If you can! All things are possible to him who believes" (9:23).

The domestic church—our homes, the primary place of learning the faith—should bring into the faith the beauty of Mother Church. Holy water, incense, holy images—all beautiful things we see in our Church—can in some way be brought into our homes to sanctify them.

Sacramentals are an outward sign of the grace bestowed through the sacraments and can become conduits for the miraculous. Sacramentals are always linked to the prayer of the Church, and those properly and rightly disposed receive graces and blessings being conferred through the object. In this book, we have already encountered many different ways to experience the invisible God through visible sacramentals, including medals, crucifixes, sacred images, blessings, and prayers. I will now look at four sacramentals we encounter in the sacred liturgy that we can bring into our homes: holy water, holy oil, incense, and candles.

Holy Water

It is the invisible reality of God's presence we get to witness with our senses when in our baptism the holy water washes, cleanses, and purifies us from original sin, welcoming us into the family of God. The same holy water used for baptism can be brought into our homes to bless us and remind us of our baptismal graces. When instructing Faithy on how to bless herself using holy water, I could finally help her remember the four places to touch on her body during the blessing. A peek in the mirror, where she could see the wet dots on her forehead, chest (right in front of her heart), and shoulders, followed by dragging a finger between them all to create the cross shape, finally linked the seemingly random actions to meaningful prayer.

Only a priest or deacon can bless water and make it holy. (We once had an elderly priest friend who used to tease that he made holy water by boiling the hell out of it. I love priest humor—it's kind of like "Dad jokes," only holier.) We keep a holy water font by our front door, hoping that those who enter will bless themselves, that anyone leaving our home will take a blessing with them, and that we'll be reminded how God works in their lives to protect, guide, and love them, even outside of the church building's walls. Finally, holy water can be used in the blessing of other sacramentals, which are not themselves efficacious in the same way as sacraments.

The Paschal Candle

Candles are often lit for special occasions—for instance, adding candles to the top of birthday cakes. (You can guess where I, as a person with mysophobia, stands on this gross tradition. Seriously, I don't know who started that, but they should be ashamed of themselves!) However, in the Catholic faith, there is also a beauty and a strong spiritual significance to the use of candles.

The Paschal candle is a sign that Jesus is the Light of the World (Jn 8:12). In our parish, the congregation gathers around a small fire kindled in a barrel in front of the church to begin the Easter Vigil liturgy. The fire is blessed, and it is from that fire that the Paschal candle is lit as a sign of the risen life of Christ. There is such a profound beauty to watching the dark church slowly illuminate solely from candlelight, as the flame is passed candle to candle, parishioner to parishioner. The Paschal candle is then brought into the church, where it remains near the altar for the next year.

At each baptism, a small candle is lit from the Paschal candle as parents and godparents, in fact, the whole Christian community, symbolically pass on the light of Christ to the new member of God's family. How amazing to call our baptism to mind every time we see the flickering flame of a candle, reminding us that ultimately it is not we who pass on the light but Christ who allows us to share in his own light and rescues us from the power of sin and darkness.

Leave a Light On

I don't think I've ever been in a church without a candle stand with candles one could light for an intention—a place to leave your prayer and your burdens behind at the altar of the Lord, knowing even when you leave that church, your prayers remain as the candle continues to burn. This simple act is an act of great trust in the love and promises of God to hear and answer our pleas.

In my parish, the candle stand is located under an image of Our Lady of Guadalupe. One of my favorite pictures of Faithy and me was one secretly taken by my husband after the two of us had lit a candle and kneeled together before the Blessed Mother to pray for her intercession. One Sunday, out of motherly curiosity, I inquired about her prayer request. She shared she prays for her brothers, who have stopped attending Mass with us. It makes her sad because she wants them to be there with her and to know Jesus. *Oh, sweet girl*, I thought, *it makes their momma sad too.*

Especially when we first brought Faithy to Mass, I must also admit to using her excitement at placing our three dollars in the box and then lighting a candle at the end of Mass as bribery to assure attentive behavior at Mass. For the first year after her adoption, we struggled with her misbehaving horrendously during Mass. Even without having a genuine concept of sound, she seemed to know that this was a place where we needed her to be quiet. She'd vocalize and squirm and throw tantrums throughout the service. We tried sitting as far away from the altar as we could, so as not to disrupt the priest and beautiful liturgy. I tried to interpret the Mass for her as best I could, even though her understanding of ASL was limited.

We tried distractions with church-appropriate, quiet toys, books, and coloring pages—unlike when I brought my son his Fisher-Price Tap & Turn, which at home on the rug was so quiet and kept him entertained for hours but on the wooden pew was not quite the same—#liveandlearn. Nothing appeased Faithy or helped us express the importance or grandeur of what was happening before her. She'd even close her eyes to block me out completely! My older boys, both hearing, expressed their jealousy at their sister's ability to shut Mom out, especially when being disciplined. I am embarrassed to say that on more than one occasion, I had to gently pry one eye open to sign "No," so she'd know—in no uncertain terms—that this response was unacceptable. (Although, the first time she did it, I was impressed with her ingenuity; how many of us can't think of at least one situation we'd love the ability to block from our lives simply by closing our eyes?)

After having to remove her from Mass more than once and count-less novenas and prayers for wisdom, I finally figured out what to do: we moved to the front pew, where I pushed aside my discomfort and self-consciousness and began interpreting so that she could see both me *and* the altar. She was fascinated by the preparation of the altar for consecration, the cleaning of the vessels afterward, and all that happens in between. Her disruptive behavior had originated not from wanting to leave but from her frustration at wanting to see more and to be nearer to the action. Although we began to see a significant change in her church behavior, I still kept the old candle-lighting treat in my parenting back pocket, just in case.

We visited shrines of many different saints in different states and tried to find particular saint statues in the Basilica of the National Shrine of the Immaculate Conception in Washington, DC, one of my favorite places in the world. I bring my petitions before each saint for their intercession. I light the candle leaving behind a reminder to me that even after I walk away, these great intercessors continue to pray for my intentions. As I ascertained from Ephesians (6:18), "Pray at all times in the Spirit, with all prayer and supplication. To that end keep alert with all perseverance, making supplication for all the saints." Therefore, I know that the more people I bring into my prayer request, whether in heaven or on earth, the more strength I will find and peace I will acquire.

I know that a candle is not a magic wand that I can light and get what I want, but the answer to every prayer I've ever prayed has begun with a sense of peace in my heart knowing that God has a purpose and a plan of sheer goodness; as the *Catechism* tells us, he has my ultimate good in his mind (*CCC* 1). God's answer to my prayers is not about my temporal welfare but my eternal one, and even though I may want certain things or believe I know how things should go, I'm bound by faith to trust: "Those who trust in him will understand truth, and the faithful will abide with him in love, because grace and mercy are upon his elect, and he watches over his holy ones" (Ws 3:9).

The Church/Home Sacramental Connection

Lourdes Water

Although I knew of the apparition and healing power of the water at Lourdes, I'd never encountered any until Kevin came home with a bottle from his men's group at the church. In a crazy *godcidence*, I'd read that same week about the miraculous powers of the water with my faith sharing group. Author Elizabeth Ficocelli described little Bernadette Soubirous's discovery of the water: "As a confirmation for her faithfulness to the lady, a spring of water soon bubbled forth from the place where Bernadette had been digging, within twenty-four hours miracles began to be reported as a result of the water."[1] The "lady" was the Blessed Virgin Mary, and that water continues to bubble up and provide miracles to this day.

Kevin gathered a small puddle of the water in his palm, dipped his index finger in it, and blessed Faith's forehead, each ear, and throat. He then invited her and I to wet our index fingers and bless ourselves with the Sign of the Cross. I'm not sure why we always feel obliged to test the miraculous power of each sacramental on Faith's ears, but we see no harm in trying. As I've stated before, we are not trying to change our daughter; however, it seems only prudent to see if the Lord wills to open her ears to hear. At the very least, the child has been thoroughly blessed over her sixteen years!

St. Joseph Oil

St. Joseph Oil is not a magic potion but a simple devotion, a "gesture of faith," as the St. Joseph's Oratory website refers to it. The tradition began with Congregation of Holy Cross Brother André Bessette. He was inspired by a practice that began in France. Taking a bit of oil from a lamp that was burning in front of a statue of St. Joseph, he then offered it to sick people, telling them to rub it on their aching bodies, bless their families with it, and pray to St. Joseph for relief and blessings.

"This tradition continues today at Saint Joseph's Oratory of Mount Royal. A basin containing ordinary vegetable oil is fixed in front of a statue of St. Joseph, and a wick, floating on the surface, burns night and day as a kind of perpetual votive lamp. The oil is then put in bottles and made available to pilgrims."[2] The oil, as with everything these days, can be purchased from the oratory's online store. A word of caution: unless you can read French, be careful checking out; but should you make a mistake and perhaps set your order to be picked up in Montreal, the oratory gift shop staff is super kind and helpful.

Incense

Our sense of smell, when considering ways to engage with our faith, seems to fly under the radar. Sure, often our church is filled with the fragrant aroma of fresh flowers, but it is the wafting smoke from the burning of incense that truly screams church! We've used the visual of the billowing smoke lifting to the heavens to illustrate our prayers raising to heaven. As described in Revelation, "and the smoke of the incense rose with the prayers of the saints from the hand of the angel before God" (8:4).

St. Bernadette Soubirous

Bernadette Soubirous, born in Lourdes, France, on January 7, 1844, "had a lively, spontaneous and generous nature; she was witty and incapable of deception."[3] She also struggled with ill health, including asthma, her entire life. She struggled to retain her catechism lessons and was unschooled until age fourteen, yet possessed a desire to know God, working hard to gain the knowledge necessary to receive her first Communion in June 1858.

On February 11, 1858, while in search of firewood, Bernadette heard a sound "like a gust of wind," and saw a light, a presence. Confused and unsure of what she was witnessing, she turned to God and took up her rosary.

The Blessed Mother visited Bernadette eighteen times, and each time she led Bernadette in the prayer of the Rosary. Interestingly, Mary only joined in reciting the Glory Be at the end of each decade. The Blessed Mother does not explain why she remained silent during the Our Father or Hail Mary; however, it seems reasonable to conjecture first the humble Mary would not pray to herself, nor because of the singular grace allotted to her by God, would have any reason to utter, "pray for us, sinners." Also of note during these visits, Our Lady of Lourdes spoke these thought-provoking words to St. Bernadette: "I do not promise you happiness in this world but in the next."

The final visit occurring on the feast of Our Lady of Mt. Carmel, July 16, 1858. The Lady, Bernadette explained, had instructed her to have a chapel built on the spot of the visions. There, the people were to come to wash in and drink of the water of the spring that had welled up from the very spot where Bernadette had been instructed to dig, where muddy water bubbled up and within a day ran clear and plentiful, during one of the appearances.

According to Bernadette, the Lady of her visions wore a white robe with a blue sash. Yellow roses covered her feet, and a large rosary was on her right arm. In the vision on March 25, she told Bernadette, "I am the Immaculate Conception." It was only when the words were explained to her that Bernadette came to realize who the Lady was.

Overwhelmed by the spotlight in Lourdes, she, along with forty-two other candidates, joined the Sisters of Charity in Nevers on July 29, 1866. There Bernadette would learn to read and write; and lived out the remainder of her thirty-five years as Sr. Marie Bernard. Bernadette is one of a few saints who became deaf later in life; she relied on basic signs for day-to-day communications with the sisters in her order.[4] Her saintly feast day was initially specified as February 18 because it was on that date that Mary expressed her promise to make Bernadette happy, not in this life but in the other. However, it is now observed in most places on the date of her death, April 16.[5]

Adopting a More Tangible Faith

Growing in Grace with Scripture

> For I received from the Lord what I also delivered to you,
> that the Lord Jesus on the night when he was betrayed took
> bread, and when he had given thanks, he broke it, and said,
> "This is my body which is for you. Do this in remembrance
> of me." In the same way also the cup, after supper, saying,
> "This cup is the new covenant in my blood. Do this, as
> often as you drink it, in remembrance of me." For as often
> as you eat this bread and drink the cup, you proclaim the
> Lord's death until he comes.
>
> Whoever, therefore, eats the bread or drinks the cup
> of the Lord in an unworthy manner will be guilty of pro-
> faning the body and blood of the Lord. Let a man exam-
> ine himself, and so eat of the bread and drink of the cup.
> For any one who eats and drinks without discerning the
> body eats and drinks judgment upon himself. That is why
> many of you are weak and ill, and some have died. (1 Cor
> 11:23–30)

Eucharist means "Thanksgiving." Honestly, I can't think of anything
that I am more grateful for in my life than the Eucharist; next comes
my husband and my children. Next, of course, is my heavenly family,
both in lineage and adopted in patronage, who buoy me on with their
prayers and example from their lives of grace, how they practiced the
faith and passed it on to me through their model. I pray I can do the
same for my family; although my older two children are currently not
practicing the faith, I know in my heart I've done everything I can to
plant the seeds, which is all we can do. I can't forget that I, too, was
away from the Catholic faith for almost ten years, during which time
the foundation laid within my heart during my years of faith formation, though dormant, was still there.

As I continue to bring the Church home to my sons from these
practices of our faith brought into our domestic church, a little Jesus
may be absorbed into their lives (unless they figure out how to do the
Faithy trick of closing her eyes and literally blocking out the entire

world). Although they don't receive Communion, I pray I can in some way bring grace to our home through my belief, reverence, and reception of the Eucharist. I long to be a channel of grace and to see them one day participating in the divine life instilled in their souls through baptism.

While sacramentals do not confer grace directly as do the sacraments, they are small, tangible, and effective ways to till the soil of our faith so we may be fertile ground, ready to receive the fullness of all the graces and blessings that God has for us. And, in turn, be witnesses of this grace to others.

Uncovering Grace

1. How has God resolved a prayer request in a way you never could have imagined? What was your initial response to his answer? Did it help you to grow closer to him, or did it take a little while to come around to the plan, especially if it meant a delay or enduring temporary suffering?
2. How do you bring the devotions and sacramentals seen in Mass into your home—your domestic church? Share how you use these for special occasions or in your everyday life.
3. We've barely skimmed the surface of how sacramentals, available through the Catholic faith, can bless our lives, and I pray you will continue to explore. Each chapter has discussed many avenues to follow to grow your own faith through these devotions. In what ways can you utilize or share them with others as a vehicle for evangelization and discipleship?

Grace-Building Activities

- Purchase a holy water font, and place it near the door of your home. Just as we bless ourselves entering the church before Mass as a sign of renewing our baptism, we can make the Sign of the Cross with holy water every time we enter our homes. It is also a perfect reminder to bring Jesus with us when we leave our homes.
- Bless your house, car, kids, and pets often with holy water. Invite a priest or deacon to offer a more formal blessing of these items.

Arrange with your priest or deacon to have holy objects such as prayer cards, Bibles, rosaries, or medals blessed after Mass or at their convenience.[6]

- Build a holy family campfire. Add a little incense to the flames, and then share prayer requests as you watch the smoke symbolically raising your prayers to heaven. You can use the time to pray the Rosary, and if you are musical (or even if you're not—like a good parent, God will think it sounds wonderful regardless), break out the Christian praise and worship songs.

- Make beeswax candles. There are many ways to do so, including buying sheets of beeswax and rolling them around a wick. There are also kits and examples online (always on Pinterest!). You can include pins, transfers, and even dried flowers to decorate for a special liturgical feast or solemnity, such as applying dried roses for St. Thérèse or creating your own mini-Paschal candle (which is a great teaching tool for children).

- Burn a candle on the anniversary of your baptism. You can use a homemade candle (or even better, find and burn your original baptismal candle), say a special prayer, sing "Happy Birthday" into the family of God, and maybe even bake a cake to celebrate. Pope Francis in his Sunday Angelus on January 10, 2016, stressed the importance of both knowing and celebrating the day of our baptism, "the date of our rebirth as children of God." He said, "I ask you a question: who among you remembers the day of their baptism?" He then urged all who did not remember to do the necessary research to find out the date, so they can celebrate this important day. He added, "Celebrating that day means and reaffirms our adherence to Jesus, with the commitment to live as Christians, members of the Church and of a new humanity, in which all are brothers and sisters."

10

A Modern-Day Miracle

St. Gemma Galgani and Religious Medals

I greatly rejoice that time flies so quickly, because that means so much less time to spend in this world, where there is nothing to attract me. My heart goes incessantly in search of a Treasure, an immense Treasure that I do not find in creatures; a Treasure that will satisfy me and console me, and give me rest.
—*St. Gemma Galgani*

Saintly Prayer Examples

I have learned many of my best faith practices from the lives of the saints. I am fascinated by the devotions and religious practices they incorporated into their lives. One of my favorite prayers is the Efficacious Novena to the Sacred Heart of Jesus, another treasured prayer card Mrs. Profetty passed down to me along with the St. Thérèse novena card. Padre Pio offered this prayer every day for the intentions given to him to pray for others. Over the years, I have experienced many unexpected and extraordinary outcomes from praying this powerful novena regarding financial burdens, difficult decisions, health woes, and so much more.

I continue to be intrigued when I discover saints who either share a devotion I love or event more remarkable, had their very own saint posse!

Sometimes the saints I uncover share both. That would be the case with St. Gemma Galgani, who would eventually become an important member of Faithy's saint posse. Gemma credited the Sacred Heart novena along with the intercession of St. Margaret Mary Alacoque, who brought the Sacred Heart devotion to the Church (see chapter 5) with her miraculous healing from meningitis.[1] She also demonstrated how sometimes answered prayers, especially miraculous ones, require a team effort. As Venerable Reverend Germanus, CP, explained it, "Gemma's cure was as perfect as it was instantaneous the Sacred Heart of Jesus being its author; Blessed Margaret Mary the intercessor, and Blessed Gabriel of the Dolours the instrument."[2] However, I knew none of this until Faithy received a very startling diagnosis.

Faithy's Little Miracle

In October 2018, at the age of twelve, Faithy received an entirely unexpected scoliosis diagnosis when her doctor found what is known as an S plus one curvature in her spine. Faithy's back curved like a slithering snake, with a fifty-degree curve, then forty-eight degrees, and ending with another twenty-eight-degree curve. The most frightening news came with the very real (and scary) possibility of spine surgery. As an adopted child, with absolutely no family medical history, procedures requiring anesthesia become even more unsettling to worried parents.

In November 2018, within a month of the diagnosis, Faithy began wearing a Boston brace. Accustoming her to wearing the brace for the prescribed eighteen hours a day was painful (for both her and us—okay, to be fair, mostly for her). Our brave girl, however, shed fewer tears than her father and I did watching her wean into this contraption and adjust to daily life, including attending school and sleeping, in a brace. Our hearts ached as our sweet, complacent child endured hours of discomfort and pain. While she eventually found some normalcy in brace life, the possible impending surgery weighed heavy on our minds. Desperate to help her, we did what any saint loving, novena praying Catholic parents might do: along with our friends' and family's prayers, we searched for a heavenly helper—a saint who could become her spiritual advocate and intercede in her hour of great need.

My deacon husband did a thorough Google search and found St. Gemma Galgani. St. Gemma, like Faithy, had been orphaned. Additionally (and quite remarkably), they would both share experiencing hearing loss and a spine curvature. While Faithy was born profoundly deaf, Gemma lost her hearing due to meningitis—the same disease that caused Gemma's spine to curve and led to her also sporting a back brace! Wow! Seriously, this is one of the things about the Catholic faith I love the most—seemingly always being able to find someone to add to our saint posse who can not only intercede for us but also empathize with our circumstances because they too experienced them.

Kevin and I began a novena to St. Gemma; in addition to miraculous healing, we had some other minor prayer requests regarding the brace situation. We needed help for Faithy at school during the weaning process since the brace could not be kept on the entire ten-plus hours she's away from home each day. The day after we began the novena, the school's physical therapist called to tell me she had worked at the very orthopedic office that not only fitted Faithy with her Boston brace but was actually the office where the design of the brace originated. She would be able to help Faithy with her brace needs at school (a huge concern weighing on our hearts), she said, adding that she was so familiar with the braces she could "put them on in her sleep." I had to hold back tears as relief washed over me. Thank you, St. Gemma!

The next heavenly assist came when we returned to the orthopedic office in December 2018, for advice on how to help her reach the magic eighteen-hour number needed for the brace to be of maximum assistance. Faithy saw a new technician, who made dramatic changes to her brace, and within a week, she was at eighteen-plus hours. She was finally able to sleep in it as well as wear it all day at school—a huge relief, as the brace, the doctor continually exhorted, only works if it is on her body!

And work it did! The third and most dramatic miraculous result came in February 2019. Just as scoliosis is considered idiopathic (with no known cause), the remarkable reduction of her two major curves to thirty degrees after only four months was also without explanation! In October when the doctor prescribed the Boston brace, he made it very clear to us, it was designed to hold the curve in hopes of keeping it from progressing. Although there are a few reported cases of improvement, results like Faithy's are not the norm. The broad smile on this usually stoic medical professional divulged without him speaking the words—he too recognized something miraculous had occurred!

Surgery, unless she chooses it in the future for cosmetic reasons, is off the table. The school physical therapist said, "So happy Faith beat the odds." We, of course, were quick to credit the incredible power of prayer, accompanied by the medical intervention, for bringing about what we consider to be a modern-day miracle.

More in Common, Maybe?

St. Gemma Galgani spoke with and saw her guardian angel, a fact I learned on the Feast of the Guardian Angels on October 2, 2020. Faithy has also indicated to me that she converses with her guardian angel, though not quite in the dramatic fashion St. Gemma did. When I first saw Faithy, at only eight years old, engaging alone in a dialog in ASL, I was intrigued but figured she was just talking to herself. I tried to respect her privacy and not "eyes drop" (the equivalent of eavesdropping on a spoken conversation). After months of witnessing these full-blown, sometimes lengthy exchanges, my curiosity piqued, I had to inquire to whom she was speaking. You can imagine my awe and amazement when she revealed it was her guardian angel. Although we'd looked at books about angels, I don't think she knew enough at the time to conjure such a fanciful story. Although I cannot prove it, I would not be surprised if this sweet, innocent girl did indeed have an extra special friendship with an angel!

Faith's Prayers for Me

Every now and then, parents get a little nugget of hope that they've done something right in their parenting. Confirmation that we've been able to impart any of our beloved faith to our daughter, longed for and always welcomed, comes in sweet gestures, moments we'll miss if we aren't keen to them. While writing this book, I took to our back deck with a notebook and Bible (I am an old-fashioned "pen to paper to computer" type of writer). Faithy joined me, so I encouraged her to go fetch paper and markers to draw, one of her favorite things. Obediently, she returned with a large pad and began diligently writing in unison with me. One of my favorite traits of hers, which of course is completely pride-driven, is how even into her teens, she enjoys copying what her father and I are doing.

Eventually, I felt her stare. Somewhat well trained not to bother Mom when she's got her head down and pen moving, Faithy had patiently waited for my attention. She then handed me her pad with a beaming smile and signed, "I wrote you a prayer to Fr. Peyton." The prayer read: "Mom need help you feets hurt some. Jeuse [Jesus], God, and Parick [Patrick] Peyton, all think help people. You sick no come sad some house," accompanied by a small picture of the three of them on an altar at our house. Her language was primitive because of her cognitive disability, but as her mom and with a little clarification from her in ASL, I could see that her writing revealed her beautiful, simple, but powerful understanding of intercessory prayer. Aware of how much I suffer because of dyshidrotic eczema, especially flares on the soles of my feet, she had brought her caring concerns to those she knew could help. Faithy's prayer ended with "No more sick people, especially mom, in our house." Amen!

Another Posse Member for Faithy: St. Francis de Sales

On January 24, we celebrate the Feast of St. Francis de Sales, a very holy and wide-reaching intercessor. The list of his patronage is extensive; however, it does not include my husband's horrible attempt at being funny, suggesting that he is the patron of shopping. (Get it? de Sales. The Sales. I know, *groan*.) Interestingly, there are quite a few topics I turn to his help with because of his patronage of authors, writers, journalists, and media due to his incredibly forward-thinking work to evangelize France through pamphlets. One of his titles particularly close to my heart is patron of the deaf.

I first learned of St. Francis's connection to the deaf the year before we adopted our daughter, while at a conference where I met the wonderful brothers (and one father) of the Oblates of St. Francis de Sales from Pennsylvania. The brothers were selling cards featuring the gorgeous artwork of their fellow Oblate Brother Mickey McGrath, OSFS. They introduced me the story of Martin, a "poor deaf mute" whom St. Francis de Sales taught the faith through a signing system they created together. That St. Francis did whatever was necessary to make the sacraments available to this young man captivates my heart, as I have encountered a similar experience as I teach my daughter the Catholic faith and prepare her to receive her sacraments through the use of ASL.

Here is an account of their sharing of faith together as told in *The Spirit of St. Francis de Sales* by the Curé of St. Sulpice:

> When he [Martin] desired to go to confession, he would enter the bishop's [St. Francis's] room, lead him into the chapel, make a motion to all who happened to be there to leave and then close all the doors and windows; finally, he would kneel down and by signs tell what he had done wrong, all the time weeping and striking his breast. The saintly confessor would mingle his tears with those of his penitent and encourage him by signs to lead a holy life and to have confidence in God.[3]

St. Francis's heart for the deaf has undoubtedly followed him into heaven. In 2013, while traveling with the Boston Deaf Apostolate for World Youth Day, I had the great blessing of seeing that firsthand. Through more saintly interventions too lengthy to share here, my son Ian and I were able to travel to Rio de Janeiro with this group to help me learn how to interpret the Mass in ASL. Traveling with us was a sweet teenage boy who was deaf and autistic. Upon arrival in Rio, he had only one desire—securing a gigantic Brazilian flag that he could wrap around himself.

He tried unsuccessfully for several days to trade the rubber wristbands we'd brought for the international exchange of gifts that happens during World Youth Day, but he couldn't find a willing participant. One morning I remembered I had packed a deck of Don Bosco playing cards given to me by a friend who had secured them during her time with Salesian sisters. I grabbed them out, brought them over to this young man, told him all about Don Bosco, shared my idea about trying to use them to barter, and told him I'd pray that the cards would bring him success in securing his much-longed-for flag.

After the morning catechesis session, he set out for lunch with several other pilgrims in our group. Tired of being wet and cold, I chose to stay behind and eat lunch in the Vivo Rio.

At three o'clock, they all came rushing in, with my friend at the front of the pack, *wrapped in the Brazilian flag*! The cards had worked! Well, really, prayer had worked, but to whose intercession could this miraculous occurrence be attributed? St. John Bosco or maybe St. Francis de Sales, patron saint of the deaf, who just happened to be the inspiration for Don Bosco's order—the Salesians! We truly are living among the Communion of Saints!

You Deserve a Medal

To honor my faithful saint friends, and to (literally) keep them close to my heart, I wear medals with the images of the saints with whom I've found favor. As the posse grew, the weight of a necklace became a bit daunting (think, Catholic Mr. T), so I moved these saintly medals onto bracelets. Some were incorporated into rosary bracelets, which included the fifty-plus beads required to pray an entire rosary. These creations were developed by my sweet friend, Laure Lynch, beginning in 2016. We had begun to experiment with "Saint Posse Bracelets," however, the dream never materialized with her untimely passing in April 2021. We did manage to create one prototype for Faithy, which included St. Gemma, a Guardian Angel, St. Francis de Sales, and the Holy Family.

St. Gemma Galgani

St. Gemma Galgani was born on March 12, 1878, in a small Italian town near Lucca, Italy.Gemma wished to become a nun, but her poor health prevented her from being accepted. She was a suffering (or victim) soul, who offered her ailments, pains, and suffering for the reparation of the sins of others and the conversion of sinners.

On June 8, 1899, Gemma had an internal locution that she'd be granted extraordinary graces to live out this suffering for the sanctification of others. She received the marks of the stigmata, manifesting as pain and blood coming from her hands, feet, and heart. Although cured of the meningitis, she remained fragile. In her autobiography, Gemma humbly recounted, "My angel answered me as follows: 'If Jesus afflicts you in your body, it is always to purify you in your soul. Be good.' Oh, how many times during my long illness did I not experience such consoling words in my heart! But I never profited by them."

In January of 1903, Gemma was diagnosed with tuberculosis. (Side note: for years, I thought the only way to become a saint was to die of TB, since it seemed every saint profile I read included a battle with the horrible disease.) Gemma died at age twenty-five on Holy Saturday, April 11, 1903. The parish priest in her company said, "She died with a smile which remained upon her lips, so that I could not convince myself that she was really dead."[4]

Religious Medals

These are sacred signs which bear a resemblance to the sacraments. They signify effects, particularly of a spiritual nature, which are obtained through the Church's spiritual intercession. By them men are disposed to receive the chief effect of the sacraments, and various occasions in life are rendered holy
—Constitution on the Sacred Liturgy, 60

The wearing of religious medals is a very ancient tradition in our Church. Archaeologists have discovered medals bearing the images of St. Peter and St. Paul manufactured in the second century, and those of St. Lawrence the Martyr from the fourth century. In the Middle Ages, medals were often distributed to pilgrims who visited sacred shrines such as St. Peter's, Rome; Canterbury, England; and Santiago de Compostela, Spain.

The use of religious medals as we know them today arose in the sixteenth century. Pope St. Pius V (d. 1572) began the custom of blessing religious medals and attaching an indulgence to them. For example, in 1566 he blessed medals with the image of Jesus and Mary and granted an indulgence to the faithful who wore them.

Medals bear the classification of a sacramental: they remind us of a holy person, which in turn opens us to grace to follow his or her example.[5]

Adopting a More Tangible Faith

Growing in Grace with Scripture

> Therefore, since we are surrounded by so great a cloud of witnesses, let us also lay aside every weight, and sin which clings so closely, and let us run with perseverance the race that is set before us, looking to Jesus the pioneer and perfecter of our faith, who for the joy that was set before him endured the cross, despising the shame, and is seated at the right hand of the throne of God. Consider him who endured from sinners such hostility against himself, so that you may not grow weary or fainthearted. (Heb 12:1–3)

In referencing a great cloud of witnesses, Hebrews reminds us of all the faithful men and women who came before us, examples of fidelity to Our Lord as well as of the Lord's faithfulness to us. The Communion of Saints are both models of holiness and our connection to heaven as our great intercessors. Just as all sacramentals are united to the prayer of the Church, all the faithful, living and dead, are united to Christ. We are all bound by the grace of our baptism to this family of heroic believers and saints in the making.

We the faithful, the cloud of witnesses, are the Church Militant (on earth), the Church Triumphant (in heaven), and the Church Suffering (in purgatory). I understood that more than ever when we faced Faithy's scoliosis diagnosis and surgery scare with no family history or medical background to help determine the best medical course to take should she need surgery. Although her heavenly family didn't give me any clues as to how she'd react under anesthesia, I felt their protective prayers covering us. Without the prayer of the Church behind us, supporting us, I can't imagine how we ever would have gotten through that situation.

Sacred images of the saints remind us of the importance of our living life toward holiness. They also remind us, as we look upon each of their faces, that we are not alone. With our saint posse, praying friends, and beloved dead, we are never alone; and regardless of our circumstances, we never need to lose heart.

Uncovering Grace

1. We've discussed saintly friends to journey with us, but what about faithful friends here below? What troubles or circumstances do you currently need covered in prayer? Who can you reach out to to pray with and for you? How can you foster godly friendships in your life?

2. Have you ever received a miracle (not necessarily a healing)? God bestows grace in many different situations. Can you recall a time when you were surprised or amazed by the outcome of something you prayed about?

3. How do you emulate the saints by praying for others? Have you ever considered asking for prayer requests on your social media platforms? If you have, what response have you received?

Grace-Building Activities

• Prayerfully select a patron saint for each member of the family, and purchase saint medals. Your choice may be based on name, interests, current circumstances, or affinities. Perhaps you will, like me, assemble an entire saint posse to accompany you through this life. After selecting the saints, visit a local Catholic bookstore or shrine to purchase a medal (or order online), have it blessed by a priest or deacon, and then wear it either around your neck, tucked in a pocket, or pinned on your clothes.

• Display religious medals. There are a variety of ways. Rosary bracelets can be created with beads or craft thread tied in knots. The Rosary Army website (RosaryArmy.com) has step-by-step instructions on how to create a knotted rosary. A saint medal can be affixed to the end of St. Thérèse's sacrifice beads (see appendix). Brainstorm different ways to make sure you are always carrying a holy helper or two with you.

• Create holy art with your plethora of religious medals collected over the years. You could buy a memorabilia frame and create a saint medal tree or make an elaborate holy art mosaic using saint medals and crucifixes displayed in a shadowbox (see Patti Maguire Armstrong's website [www.PattiMaguireArmstrong.com] for this amazing idea). These art pieces are a perfect addition to your prayer corner, a table, or a special space in your home. Be really bold and courageous by decorating your desk at work with it or displaying the frame front and center at the entrance of your home!

Conclusion

Conclusions are difficult to write, especially when you yearn for the reader to continue exploring the book's subject. My husband suggested I end the book with a slight variation on his favorite Christmas story with something like, "and little Faithy, who did not die." My friend quickly added I should at least include, "God bless us, everyone." Although I appreciated their suggestions, and both sentiments in some ways are appropriate to the subject, I was reasonably sure people would recognize the plagiarism. More important, it is not where I wanted to conclude this adoption story and our encounters with signs of faith.

As an icebreaker at a recent virtual gathering, I suggested the participants share their favorite sacramental. Little did I know the incredible and touching stories this question would unleash. One of my most cherished sacramentals is the petite porcelain statue of the Infant of Prague I accidentally discovered tucked and heftily glued in a dusty plastic flower patch among other treasures lovingly assembled in my godmother's home shrine. I'm not sure what draws me to this image of the child Jesus; perhaps it is the sweet face that reminds me of the promises and graces of the powerful novena associated with this devotion.

As with many sacramentals, the stories bring an even richer encounter to the devotion. I am so intrigued by the folklore around acquiring one's Infant of Prague image, either a ceramic one like mine or the fancier doll version with colorful liturgical vestments. Many believe the Infant will find you, and I've heard stories of yard-sale finds, random bequeathing, and other buried in dusty, unexpected places stories! My sweet porcelain friend sits on my shelf, peering lovingly over my shoulder as I work in Catholic ministry each day.

Devotions play an exciting role in the life of a Catholic, especially in helping to make the invisible God—visible. Secret treasures of the Church—hidden in plain sight. Devotions to literally cling to in difficult times or share with others as a means of evangelization; precious tools wrapped in a sweet story. How blessed are we to have so many ways to connect us to our truly unfathomable God. Devotions join us in worship, not, of course, the often-misunderstood accusation of idol worship, but a glorification of the Lord who gives us all that we need, including the reassurances of tangible graces. The limits of our carnal bodies crave physical reminders of God's heavenly assurances.

I invite you to reflect again on how the *Catechism of the Catholic Church* describes sacramentals, as it provides an evocative scope of sacramentals in the life of a Catholic Christian:

> Sacramentals do not confer the grace of the Holy Spirit in the way that the sacraments do, but by the Church's prayer, they prepare us to receive grace and dispose us to cooperate with it. "For well-disposed members of the faithful, the liturgy of the sacraments and sacramentals sanctifies almost every event of their lives with the divine grace which flows from the Paschal mystery of the Passion, Death, and Resurrection of Christ. From this source all sacraments and sacramentals draw their power. There is scarcely any proper use of material things which cannot be thus directed toward the sanctification of men and the praise of God. (1670)

From our wedding rings to our beloved Bibles to the heavenly images we collect around us, sacramentals continually remind us of the abundant graces God has for each of us. Graces Mother Mary relayed through St. Catherine Labouré and the Miraculous Medal, which often remain unused because we simply fail to ask for them. Surrounding myself with devotional objects acts then as a "string around my finger" so that I may never forget to seek God in every aspect and every moment of my life.

Look around you; what (or whom) do the sacred images or objects surrounding you bring to mind? What sweet stories of God's faithfulness do they evoke? These are our legacies of faith, heirlooms of hope; catechesis lived and shared instead of preached—the methodology more comfortable, natural, authentic, framed in story—as the gospels revealed Jesus did.

Rosaries passed down, even if their current state is just a pile of beads, a chain, and a worn crucifix, which describes the rosary I inherited from my father (passed down from his mother). Tattered, these beads still serve to bring me closer to Christ because looking at them reminds me of my grandmother's virtuous faith, humble heart, and faithful Sunday Mass attendance. Although not the rosary beads I clung to that homesick night so many years before, her advice to pray them when I felt homesick means even more to me now, those moments I get homesick for heaven and the peace, joy, and love that awaits me there.

At a funeral several years ago, the family placed a worn bible, tied together with a shoelace, upon the casket during the Mass of Christian Burial. What a testament to this man's faith, what a witness to all of us present of what truly mattered in his life. The Word of God sustained him as we would hear in the eulogy, but honestly, the Bible said everything—no further explanation required. My grandmother's well-worn beads, this man's ragged Bible, and so many beloved and much-used sacramentals tell a story; they tell adoption stories of faith—a faith chosen, cherished, and beloved.

My little girl is not so little anymore; as I write this, she is just a month away from her Confirmation. There is still much we have to teach her. Let's be honest; there is also something about God we have to learn. We continue to use visuals and tangibles of the faith to overcome the difficulties in comprehension her cognitive delay present. Yet, I believe with my whole heart, the Holy Spirit guides her faith in ways I'll never understand. As I see her signing away to her guardian angel or intently watching the Consecration during Mass, I am acutely aware she knows things I'll never comprehend this side of heaven. I must admit, this awareness sometimes causes me a bit of godly jealousy mixed with a mother's great relief at the same time.

I pray you, along with your family, will continue to discover the mystical beauty of the Catholic Church and a God that loves you so deeply and completely through the tangible graces of faith.

Appendix

Miraculous Medal Novena

In the name of the Father, and of the Son, and of the Holy Spirit. Amen.

Come, O Holy Spirit, fill the hearts of your faithful, and kindle in them the fire of your love. Send forth your Spirit, and they shall be created. And you shall renew the face of the earth.

Let us pray. Oh God, who did instruct the hearts of the faithful by the light of the Holy Spirit, grant us in the same Spirit to be truly wise and ever to rejoice in his consolation, through Jesus Christ, Our Lord. Amen.

O Mary, conceived without sin. Pray for us who have recourse to you. *[Repeat 3 times.]*

O Lord, Jesus Christ, who have vouchsafed to glorify by numberless miracles the Blessed Virgin Mary, immaculate from the first moment of her conception, grant that all who devoutly implore her protection on earth, may eternally enjoy your presence in heaven, who, with the Father and Holy Spirit, live and reign, God forever and ever. Amen.

O Lord, Jesus Christ, who for the accomplishment of your greatest works, have chosen the weak things of the world, that no flesh may glory in your sight; and who for a better and more widely diffused belief in the Immaculate Conception of your Mother, have wished that the Miraculous Medal be manifested to St. Catherine Labouré, grant we beseech you, that filled with like humility, we may glorify this mystery by word and work. Amen.

Memorare

Remember, O most compassionate Virgin Mary, that never was it known that anyone who fled to your protection, implored your assistance, or sought your intercession, was left unaided. Inspired with this confidence, we fly unto you, O Virgin of Virgins, our Mother; to you we come; before you we kneel, sinful and sorrowful. O Mother of the Word Incarnate, despise not our petitions, but, in your clemency, hear and answer them. Amen.

Novena Prayer

O Immaculate Virgin Mary, Mother of our Lord Jesus and our Mother, penetrated with the most lively confidence in your all-powerful and never-failing intercession, manifested so often through the Miraculous Medal, we, your loving and trustful children, implore you to obtain for us the graces and favors we ask during this Novena if they be beneficial to our immortal souls, and the souls for whom we pray.

[Include your intentions here.]

You know, O Mary, how often our souls have been the sanctuaries of your Son who hates iniquity. Obtain for us, then, a deep hatred of sin and that purity of heart which will attach us to God alone, so that our every thought, word, and deed may tend to his greater glory. Obtain for us also a spirit of prayer and self-denial, that we may recover by penance what we have lost by sin and at length attain to that blessed abode where you are the Queen of angels and of men. Amen.

An Act of Consecration to Our Lady of the Miraculous Medal

O Virgin Mother of God, Mary Immaculate, we dedicate and consecrate ourselves to you under the title of Our Lady of the Miraculous Medal. May this Medal be for each one of us a sure sign of your affection for us and a constant reminder of our duties toward you. Ever while wearing it, may we be blessed by your loving protection and preserved in the grace of your Son. O most powerful Virgin, Mother of our Savior, keep us close to you every moment of our lives. Obtain for us, your children, the grace of a happy death; so that, in union with you, we may enjoy the bliss of heaven forever. Amen.

Repeat 3 times: O Mary, conceived without sin. Pray for us who have recourse to you.[1]

Lectio Divina (Divine Reading)

Books and the internet boast no shortage of instructions for the practice of lectio divina (Latin for divine reading). The traditional four-step process for entering deeper into scripture includes reading (*lectio*), meditating (*meditatio*), praying (*oratio*), and contemplation (*contemplatio*); there are some of which I am one, who employ a fifth step, action (*actio*). Instead of explaining these steps, I find a hands-on approach more conducive for incorporating the practice into your time with the Bible.

For each verse, please pause and repeat the verse two or three times to yourself. Ask yourself questions, ponder whatever images come to mind, and consider the lesson God offers you through these words. Contemplate how to bring this scripture into your life as an action or an inspiration. I'm going to feature only a few verses, but I highly encourage you to continue to spend time with the rest of Proverbs 31. Scripture can be a perfect vehicle for increasing meaningful prayer in your life.

So let's begin first by inviting the Holy Spirit into this time of prayer and reflection:

> Come Holy Spirit, inspire the hearts of your faithful who come to you this day seeking to embrace their goodness as wife, mother, and woman. May contemplating your Word help us all to see our immeasurable worth through God's loving and merciful eyes.

Ode to a Capable Wife (Proverbs 31)

Several versions of the Bible title Proverbs 31 as "A Wife of Noble Character." The dictionary defines a noble person as one who possesses fine personal qualities or high moral principles or ideals; one who is good, righteous, and virtuous. I would venture to say many women would admit they desire, and perhaps even strive, to be a wife of noble character, yet may not feel they truly are. I'd be one of those wives. I have my not-so-noble moments in my human frailty; however, that doesn't mean you and I are not still women of great worth.

I have chosen to use the RSVCE version of the Bible, drawn to the friendlier (and encouraging) Proverbs 31 subtitle "Ode to a Capable Wife." While I struggle to see myself as noble and as worthy as God sees me, I can embrace the idea of being, at the very least, capable. Even on my worst days, my kids were fed, and no one left the house naked; I consider those major wins in the capability category!

> A good wife who can find?
> She is far more precious than jewels. (Prv 31:10)

What jewel did you picture? Can you see yourself as a clear, multifaceted, sparkling diamond? Have you considered how valuable you are to your family?

A sacramental marriage rooted in the Lord and trust is more valuable than any earthen treasure.

> She is like the ships of the merchant,
> she brings her food from afar. (Prv 31:14)

As a woman who loathes cooking, this verse concerns me. Am I less noble because I prefer the food from afar to arrive by DoorDash? Does my value diminish if our dinner bell sounds strangely the same as our fire alarm? No, my value comes from the faithfulness of my care of my family. The blessing I offer comes in my orchestrating the Peapod delivery or trudging through meal planning; I don't need to be Julia Child, mastering the art of French cooking to bless my family. A nurturing heart comes from a variety of flavors!

> She perceives that her merchandise is profitable.
> Her lamp does not go out at night. (Prv 31:18)

Like the ten virgins awaiting their bridegroom, I fill my lamp with the oil of my faith. How do you keep your lamp plied with oil? In what ways do you refill the flasks of your faith? Are you careful to make time tending your relationship with Jesus? Remember, we cannot give what we do not have, and our example is often a more powerful lesson than the words we speak.

> Strength and dignity are her clothing,
> and she laughs at the time to come. (Prv 31:25)

These past months have been filled with anxiety and uncertainty. The idea of laughing at the days to come may seem truly impossible. Maybe even a little loony. The Proverbs 31 Woman is not mad, insane, nor ignorant. She can laugh at the days to come and see them with joy because she fixes her eyes on Jesus, and it is from him that she gains her strength! She is worthy, noble, and yes, capable, of rooting her heart in Jesus's Sacred Heart and Mary's Immaculate Heart. She finds worth in her ability to surrender entirely to the One who created her and the One who makes her days. The real worth of a wife is her ability to see her strengths and weaknesses as occasions to rely on God's grace. Only in, through, and with our Triune God are any of us genuinely righteous, virtuous, or capable.

St. Thérèse's Sacrifice Beads

Supplies Needed

- 3 feet of cord (The string must fit through the bead twice. Note: a stiffer cord allows for the beads to be slid throughout the day, and then stay in place, to help you keep count of your sacrifices, prayers, or good deeds.)
- A St. Thérèse medal
- A crucifix
- Plastic, glass, ceramic, or wooden beads with large holes for stringing

How to Make Sacrifice Beads[2]

1. Begin with the St. Thérèse medal. Find the middle of the string and put it through the end of the medal. This will make a loop with the middle of the string. Take the two ends of the string and put them through the loop.
2. Pull the two ends of the string tight, and it will attach the string to the St. Thérèse medal.
3. Select ten beads and decide the order you want to string them in.
4. Take the first bead. Put one string through one side and one string through the other side.
5. Pull both ends of the string and the bead will start sliding up toward the medal or crucifix. Keep pulling the two strings in opposite directions until the bead goes all the way up to the end where you have the medal.
6. Continue stringing in the way described in steps four and five for all ten beads.
7. Leave a space and tie a double knot by wrapping the string around your fingers and putting the ends of the string through the hole. Then add the crucifix and double knot again.
8. Depending on the type of cord or string used, coating the ends in clear nail polish or slightly singeing the ends with a lighter may be required to keep them from fraying.

Efficacious Novena to the Sacred Heart

O my Jesus, you have said: "Truly I say to you, ask and it will be given you, seek and you will find, knock and it will be opened to you." Behold, I knock, I seek and ask for the grace of *[insert your intention]*. Our Father . . . Hail Mary . . . Glory be to the Father . . . Sacred Heart of Jesus, I place all my trust in you.

O my Jesus, you have said: "Truly I say to you, if you ask anything of the Father in my name, he will give it to you." Behold, in your name, I ask the Father for the grace of *[insert your intention]*. Our Father . . . Hail Mary . . . Glory be to the Father . . . Sacred Heart of Jesus, I place all my trust in you.

O my Jesus, you have said: "Truly I say to you, heaven and earth will pass away but my words will not pass away." Encouraged by your infallible words, I now ask for the grace of *[insert your intention]*. Our Father . . . Hail Mary . . . Glory be to the Father . . . Sacred Heart of Jesus, I place all my trust in you.

O Sacred Heart of Jesus, for whom it is impossible not to have compassion on the afflicted, have pity on us miserable sinners and grant us the grace which we ask of you, through the Sorrowful and Immaculate Heart of Mary, your tender Mother and ours.

Recite the **Hail, Holy Queen**:

> Hail, Holy Queen, Mother of Mercy,
> our life, our sweetness, and our hope.
> To you do we cry,
> poor banished children of Eve.
> To you do we send up our sighs,
> mourning and weeping in this valley of tears.
> Turn then, most gracious advocate,
> your eyes of mercy toward us,
> and after this exile
> show unto us the blessed fruit of thy womb,
> Jesus.
> O clement, O loving,
> O sweet Virgin Mary.

Conclude with:
> St. Joseph, foster father of Jesus, pray for us.[3]

Notes

1. All about Grace

1. Association of the Miraculous Medal, accessed May 23, 2022. https://www.amm.org/.

2. In *The How-To Book of Sacramentals: Everything You Need to Know But No One Ever Taught You*, by Ann Ball (Huntington, IN: Our Sunday Visitor, 2005). 200, Mary is quoted as saying, "Some of the precious stones gave forth no ray of light." In the apparition, Catherine recounts the jewels are on Mary's fingers and it is from them that the rays emanate.

3. "St. Catherine Labouré," The Miraculous Medal Shrine, accessed April 5, 2022, https://miraculousmedal.org/welcome/story-of-st-catherine.

4. "The Early Life of Saint Catherine Labouré," Association of the Miraculous Medal, accessed May 23, 2022, https://www.amm.org/aboutamm/story%20of%20st%20catherine.aspx.

5. "A Medal that Changed the World," Association of the Miraculous Medal, accessed May 23, 2022, https://miraculousmedal.org/the-message/a-medal-that-changed-the-world/.

6. Adapted from "History," St. Catherine Labouré Catholic Church, accessed October 30, 2021http://www.stcatherinelaboure.com/History.

7. Adapted from "Story of the Miraculous Medal," Miraculous Medal Shrine, accessed October 30, 2021, https://miraculousmedal.org/welcome/the-miracle-of-the-miraculous-medal/.

8. "The Miraculous Medal Perpetual Novena," Miraculous Medal Shrine, accessed October 30, 2021, https://miraculousmedal.org/worship-and-prayer/miraculous-medal-novena-prayers/.

2. Companions on the Journey

1. For more on Padre Pio, see chapter 3.

2. "Mary Faustina Kowalska," the Vatican, accessed May 23, 2022, https://www.vatican.va/news_services/liturgy/saints/ns_lit_doc_20000430_faustina_en.html.

3. Surrendering to the Cross

1. Frank M. Rega, *Padre Pio and America* (Gastonia, NC: TAN Books, 2008), loc. 3997 of 4615, Kindle.

2. "The Story of the Flying Monk: A Myth, a Legend or Reality?," *Italian Tribune*, April 6, 2021, https://italiantribune.com/the-story-of-the-flying-monk-a-myth-a-legend-or-reality/.

3. "The Spiritual Child of Padre Pio of Pietrelcina," devotional blog dedicated to Padre Pio, accessed May 23, 2022, https://www.padrepiodapietrelcina.com/en/spiritual-child-of-padre-pio/.

4. F. Cabrol, "The True Cross," *The Catholic Encyclopedia* (New York: Robert Appleton Company, 1908). New Advent, http://www.newadvent.org/cathen/04529a. htm, accessed May 23, 2022.

5. "Good Friday," Catholic Online, April 15, 2022, https://www.catholic.org/lent/friday.php.

4. A Little Prayer Never Hurts

1. Thérèse of Lisieux, *The Story of a Soul: The Autobiography of St. Thérèse of Lisieux*, trans. by Thomas N. Taylor (Washington: ICS Publications, 2007), 88.

2. Thérèse of Lisieux, *The Story of a Soul*, 65–66.

3. Thérèse of Lisieux, *The Story of a Soul*, 152.

5. Covered in Love

1. Emily Jaminet, *Secrets of the Sacred Heart: Twelve Ways to Claim Jesus' Promises in Your Life* (Notre Dame, IN: Ave Maria Press, 2020), ix.

2. Jaminet, *Secrets of the Sacred Heart*, 107.

3. Adapted from John Croiset, *Devotion to the Sacred Heart of Jesus: How to Practice the Sacred Heart Devotion* (Gastonia, NC: TAN Books, 2007).

4. Congregation for Divine Worship and the Discipline of the Sacraments, *Directory on Popular Piety and the Liturgy: Principles and Guidelines* (Vatican City: Vatican, 2001), 205.

5. Mike Aquilina and Regis J. Flaherty, *The How-To Book of Catholic Devotions, Second Edition* (Huntington, IN: Our Sunday Visitor, 2016), 213.

6. "Enthrone Your Home and School," Welcome His Heart, accessed May 23, 2022, https://welcomehisheart.com/enthronement.

6. My Weapon of Choice

1. Adapted from Richard Gribble, *American Apostle of the Family Rosary: The Life of Patrick J. Peyton, CSC* (Chestnut Ridge, NY: Crossroad Publishing Company, 2011).

2. Adapted from "The Rosary & St. Dominic: In Defense of a Tradition," Rosary Center & Confraternity, https://rosarycenter.org/the-rosary-and-st.-dominic, accessed October 30, 2021.

3. Adapted from Donald H. Calloway, MIC, *26 Champions of the Rosary: The Essential Guide to the Greatest Heroes of the Rosary* (Stockbridge, MA: Marian Press, 2017).

4. For information on how to pray the Our Lady Undoer of Knots Novena, see www.theholyrosary.org/maryundoerknots.

7. Inspired by the Word

1. *The Didache Bible* (San Francisco: Ignatius Press, 2015), 4150.

2. Brian Thomas Becket Mullady, *Grace Explained: How to Receive—and Retain—God's Most Potent Gift* (Irondale, AL: EWTN Publishing, 2021), chapter 10, Kindle.

8. Someone to Look Up To

1. "The Statue of St. Joseph That Pope Francis Keeps in His Room," Rome Reports, March 19, 2015, video, 1:52, https://www.romereports.com/en/2015/03/19/the-statue-of-st-joseph-that-pope-francis-keeps-in-his-room/.

2. Adapted from "Juan Diego Cuauhtlatoatzin," vatican.va, accessed May 23, 2022, https://www.vatican.va/news_services/liturgy/saints/ns_lit_doc_20020731_juan-diego_en.html.

3. Congregation for Divine Worship, *Directory on Popular Piety and the Liturgy: Principles and Guidelines* (Chicago: Pauline Books & Media, 2003), 238, 239.

9. Staying Connected to Church

1. Elizabeth Ficocelli, *Thérèse, Faustina, and Bernadette: Three Saints Who Challenged My Faith, Gave Me Hope, and Taught Me How to Love* (Notre Dame, IN: Ave Maria Press, 2014), 138.

2. "St. Joseph Oil," Saint Joseph's Oratory of Mount Royal, accessed May 23, 2022, https://www.saint-joseph.org/en/spirituality/saint-joseph/saint-joseph-oil.

3. "Bernadette Soubirous," Lourdes Sanctuaire, accessed May 23, 2022, https://www.lourdes-france.org/en/bernadette-soubirous/.

4. Lana Portolano, *Be Opened! The Catholic Church & Deaf Culture* (Washington, DC: Catholic University of America Press, 2020), 43.

5. Adapted from "Bernadette Soubirous," Lourdes Sanctuaire, accessed October 30, 2021, https://www.lourdes-france.org/en/bernadette-soubirous.

6. For more on this, see United States Conference of Catholic Bishops, *Catholic Household Blessings and Prayers*, revised and updated edition (Washington, DC: United States Conference of Catholic Bishops, 2020).

10. A Modern-Day Miracle

1. Venerable Reverend Germanus, CP, *The Life of Saint Gemma Galgani*, trans. A. M. O'Sullivan (London: Catholic Way Publishing, 2014), chapter 6, ebook.

2. Venerable Reverend Germanus, *Life of Saint Gemma Galgani*, chapter 6.

3. Quoted in "Saint Francis De Sales and Martin, Saint Francis Develops Sign Language for his Deaf Servant," The Sisters of the Visitation, January 18, 2014. https://toledovisitation.org/2014/01/saint-francis-de-sales-martin-deaf-servant/.

4. Venerable Reverend Germanus, *Life of Saint Gemma Galgani*, chapter 1.

5. Adapted from "What Is the Origin of Wearing Religious Medals?," Catholic Straight Answers, accessed October 30, 2021, https://catholicstraightanswers.com/what-is-the-origin-of-wearing-religious-medals.

Appendix

1. Adapted from the Miraculous Medal Perpetual Novena found at The Miraculous Medal Shrine, accessed May 25, 2022, https://miraculousmedal.org/worship-and-prayer/perpetual-novena/.

2. Instructions adapted from www.catholicicing.com/make-your-own-sacrifice-beads. Catholic Icing's website includes step-by-step photos and a how-to video.

3. Adapted from www.padrepio.org/pray/efficacious-novena/.

Allison Gingras is a Catholic new media consultant, supporting Family Rosary, Catholic Mom, and the Diocese of Fall River. She is the host and creator of the podcast *A Seeking Heart*.

Gingras developed and acquired six volumes in the Stay Connected Journals for Women series and wrote two—*The Gift of Invitation* and *Seeking Peace*. She is a contributor to a number of books, including *The Ave Prayer Book for Catholic Mothers*, *Called by Name*, and *The Catholic Mom's Prayer Companion*. Gingras has been featured on a variety of Catholic television and radio programs and podcasts. She is a regular contributor to LPI, Diocesan.com, CatholicMom.com, Family Rosary, WINE, Amazing Catechists, and CatholicSistas. Gingras is the cohost of the Catholic MomCast.

She was given the Light of Christ Award by the Archdiocese of Boston in 2008. She is a member of Bishop Edgar M. da Cunha's Diocesan Revitalization Committee in the Fall River Diocese. Gringras is a member of the Catholic Writers Guild, the National Council of Catholic Women, and Catholics Online.

She earned a bachelor's degree in English from Bridgewater State University and a master's degree in technology in education from Lesley University. She is a certified paralegal.

reconciledtoyou.com
Facebook: Reconciled To You
Twitter: @reconciledtoyou
Instagram: @reconciledtoyou
Pinterest: @allisongringras
YouTube: Allison Gingras

AVE

AVE MARIA PRESS

Founded in 1865, Ave Maria Press,
a ministry of the Congregation of
Holy Cross, is a Catholic publishing
company that serves the spiritual and
formative needs of the Church and its
schools, institutions, and ministers;
Christian individuals and families; and
others seeking spiritual nourishment.

For a complete listing of titles from

Ave Maria Press

Sorin Books

Forest of Peace

Christian Classics

visit www.avemariapress.com

AVE MARIA PRESS
Notre Dame, IN
A Ministry of the United States Province of Holy Cross